The Create a Character Picture Book - with extras!

Volume IV featuring art created at PWhack Con 2018.

The Create a Character Picture Book by John Graham. Published by FIGID Press
Brownsburg, IN 46112 www.FIGIDPress.com / FIGIDPress@Gmail.com
© 2018 Unique characters created are copyright to the respective creators listed. Existing characters are copyrighted to their existing companies.
All rights reserved. No portion of this book may be reproduced in any form without permission from the publisher, except as permitted by U.S. copyright law. For permissions contact:

Cover design and formatting by the talented Phil Velikan. Hire him for your next project!
Website: FindPhil.com

What is this Book?

Welcome to a celebration of art and creativity. This book contains amazing artwork completed by all ages and all skill levels, looking to share their talent with the world. In this book you'll find over fifty pages of illustrations featuring unique and existing characters done by attendees at this year's PWhack Con. These brave creators took a moment and put pencil to paper in an effort to share their love of art with you.

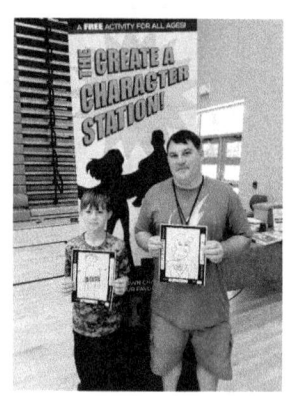

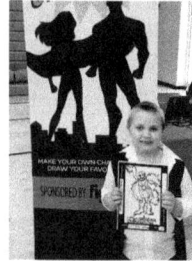

Some characters are old favorites drawn out of respect to the comic medium that has encouraged so much creativity over the years. Other pages feature completely new characters, springing from their creator's imagination just for this book.

Beyond the characters, this book also features some bonus sections to make it a special keepsake for years to come. You'll find pages to record your experiences from the show this year, along with an area for ideas for next years event. You'll find additional sketch pages so you can keep creating and perfecting your artistic craft. There's even a section featuring a variety of comic page templates for you to copy and use to create the adventures of your favorite characters.

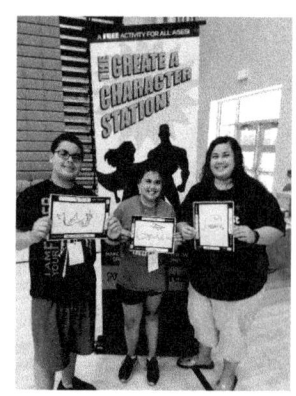

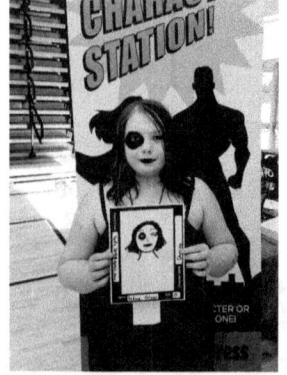

Use this book through the year as a way to improve your skill and then bring it back to the next event in the future to get feedback from the artists exhibiting there.

So flip through the pages and find the inspiration you need to get started.

The Create a Character Station

Imagine a place where you can sit down, relax, and just be creative. A place where people can give you some artistic advice or just be excited for you as you create art. A place that's open to all ages and all skill levels, looking forward to publishing pictures of their characters.

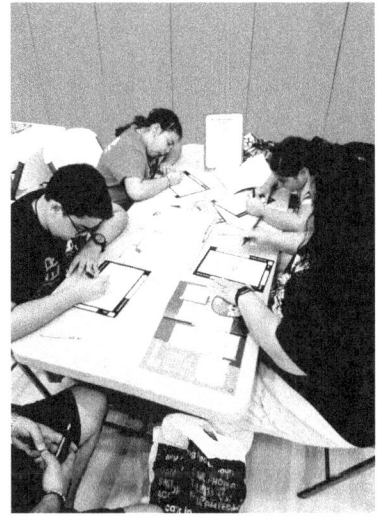

This is the **Create a Character Station,** and it will hopefully be coming to more events near you. Participants just have to sit down and start drawing. Paper, pencils, reference books, and local creators are there for use, completely free of charge.

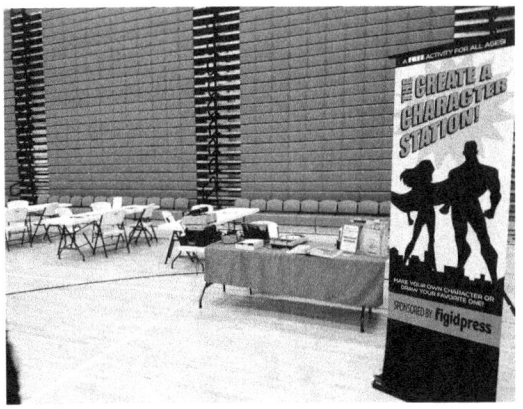

Our mission is to encourage creativity and inspire creators to keep going. We've found that there's nothing more powerful than creating something and then seeing it printed in a book.

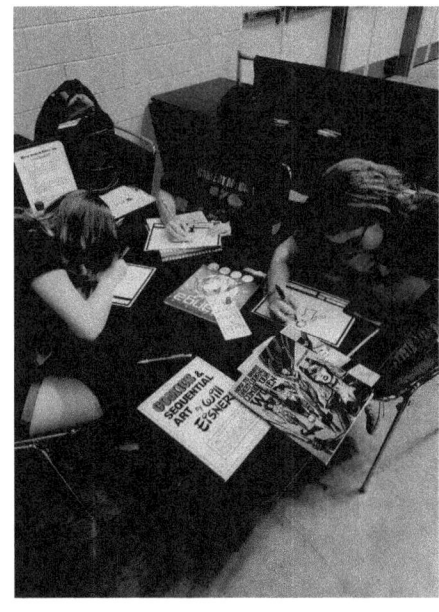

Holding and sharing your creation with others can quickly lead to the next project and then the next. Before you know it, your skill level and confidence has sky rocketed and you can't be stopped.

This book in your hands may be the first step to stardom for an aspiring artist and you just helped them get there. Thanks!

Princess Gokkiss

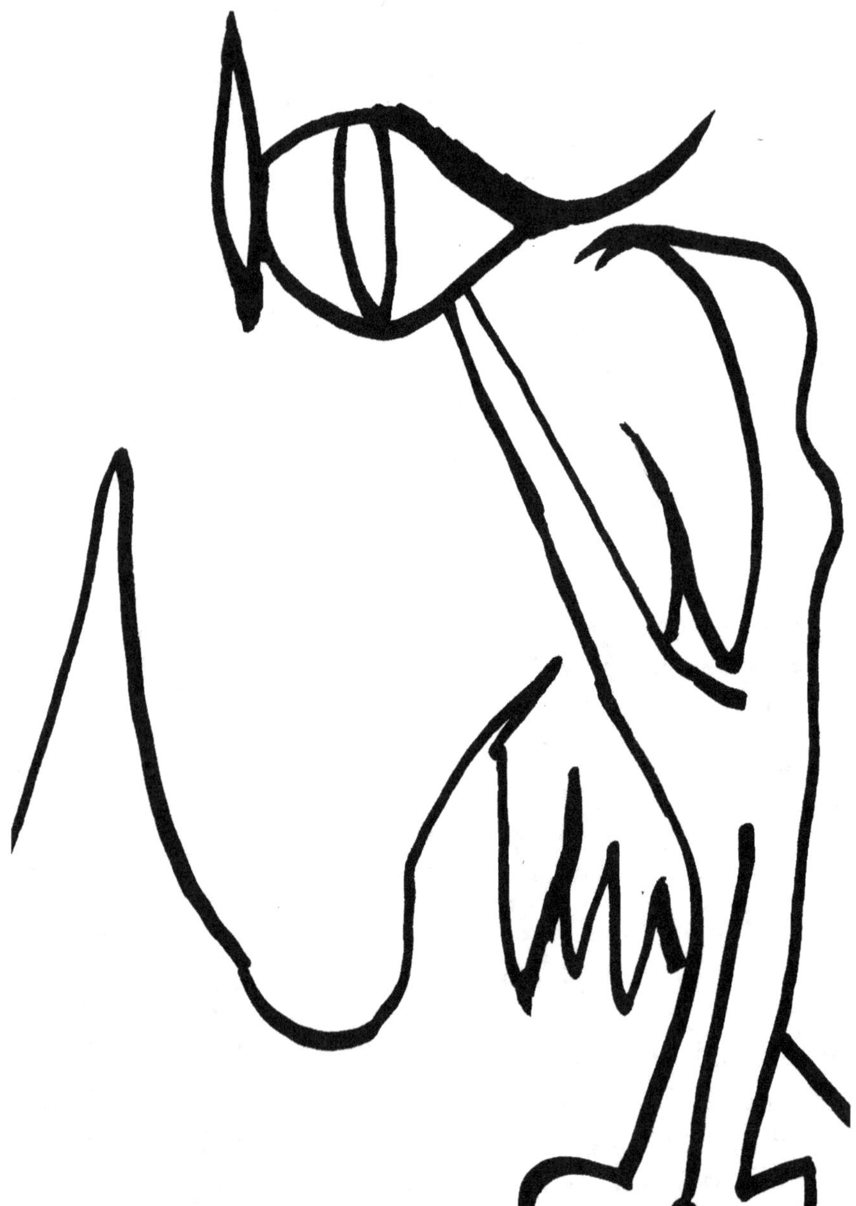

Creator Name: **Khloey**

Age: **2**

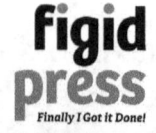

Stick Botical

Creator Name: **Elijah**

Age: **5**

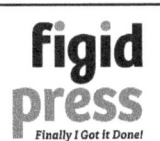

Hetaro

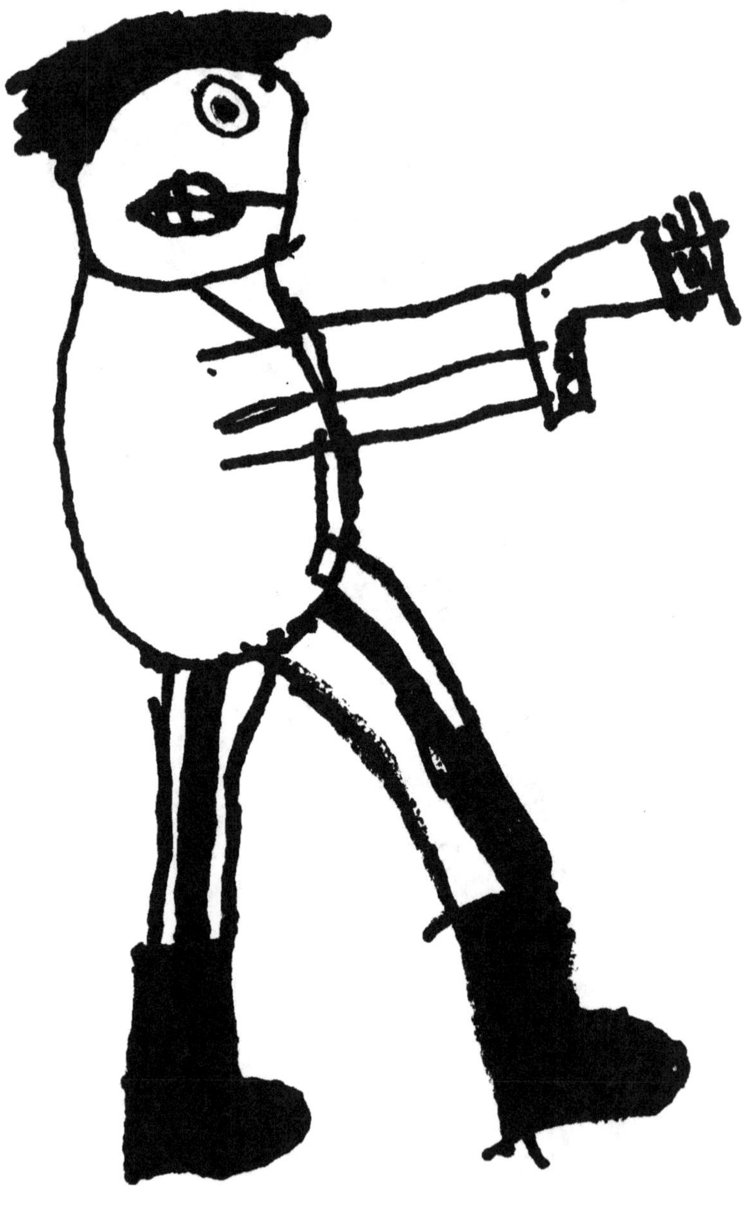

Creator Name: **Corbin Williams**

Age: **6**

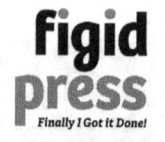

Glacier

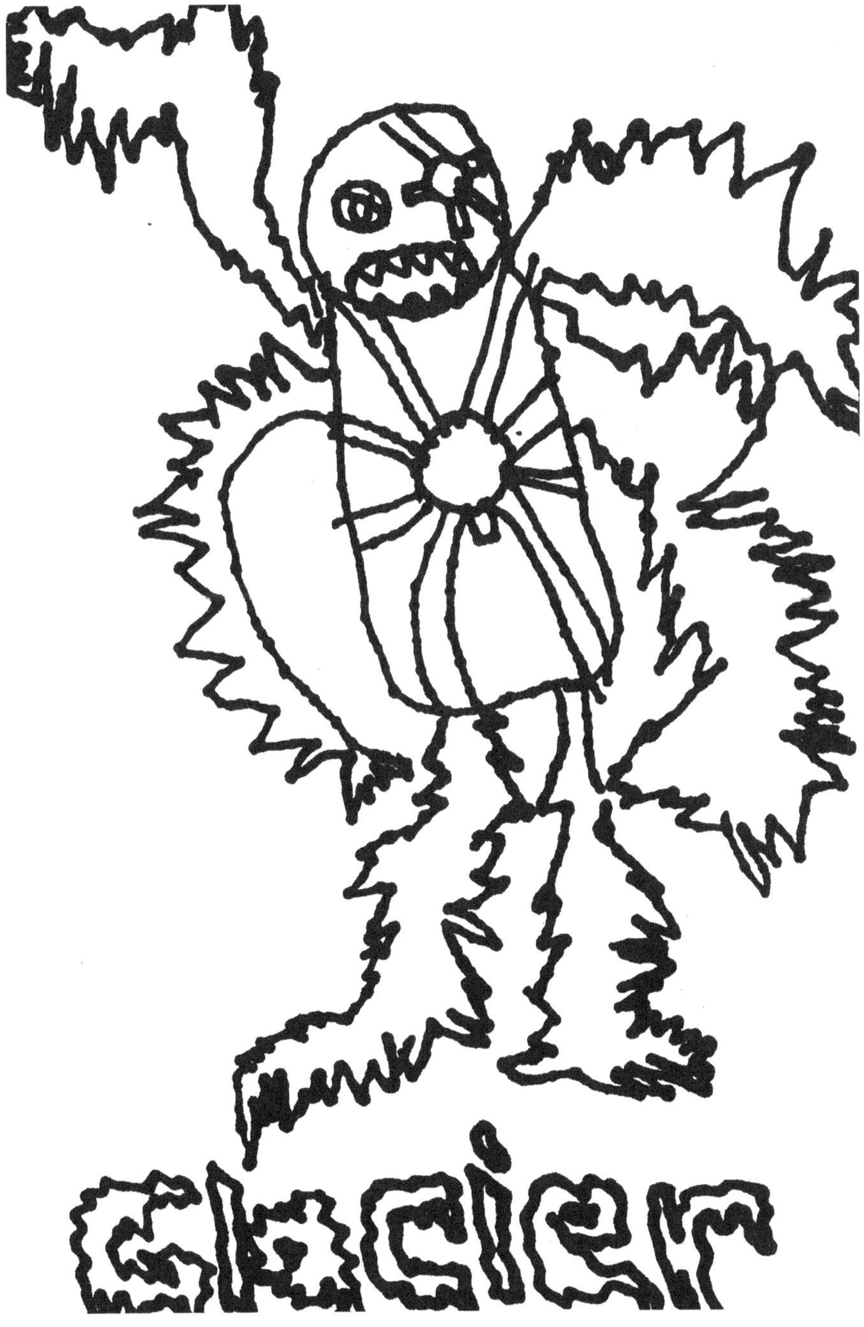

Creator Name: **Corbin Williams**

Age: **6**

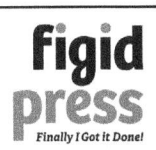

Black Panther

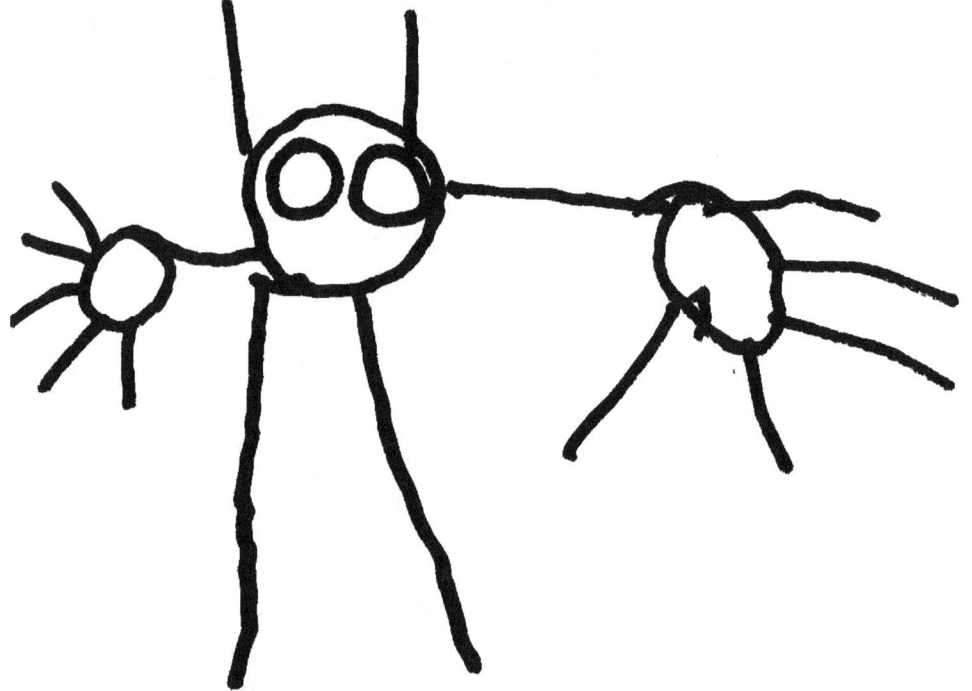

Creator Name: *Autumn Snearley*

Age: 6

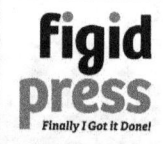

Wizard Wonko

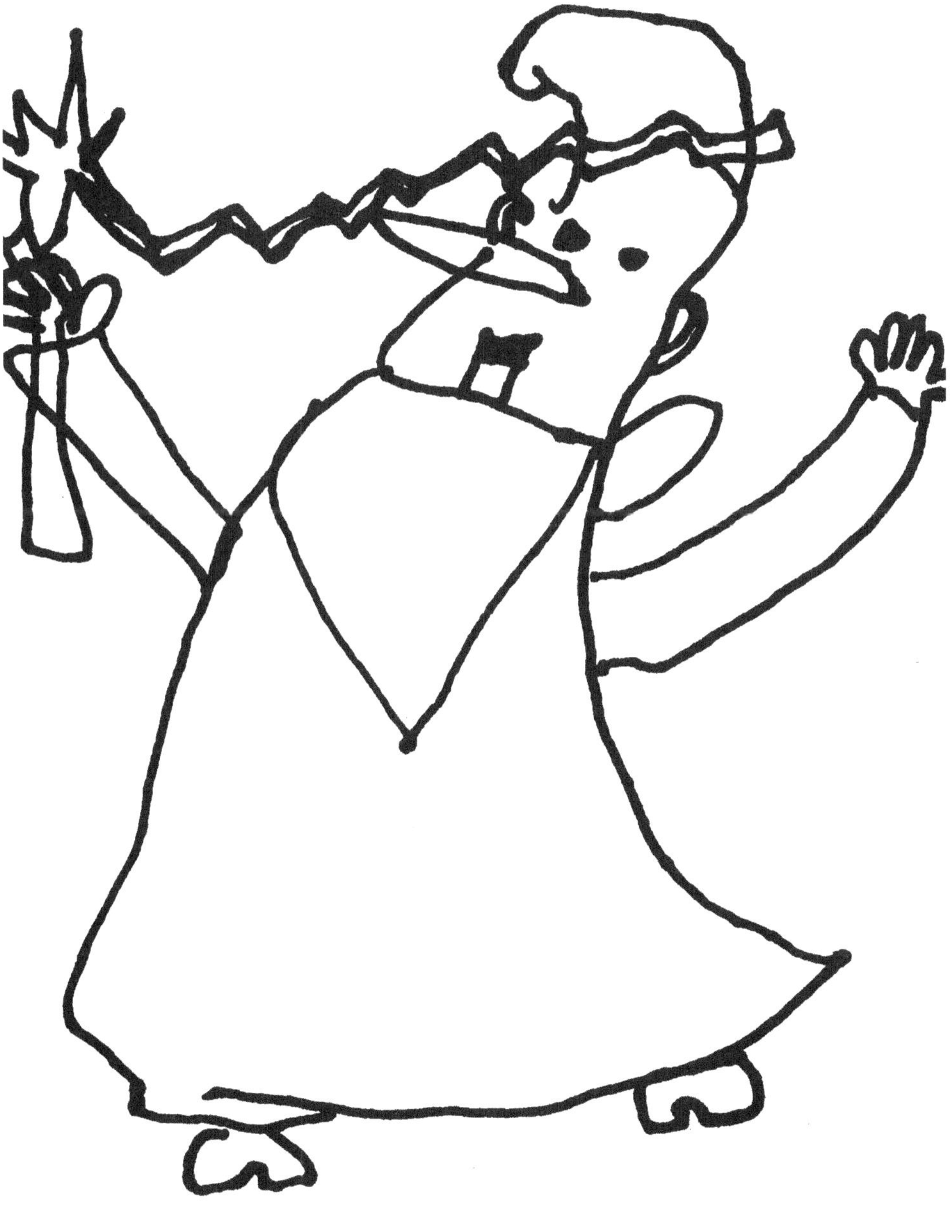

Creator Name: **Abby**

Age: **9**

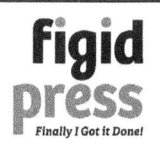

Truman

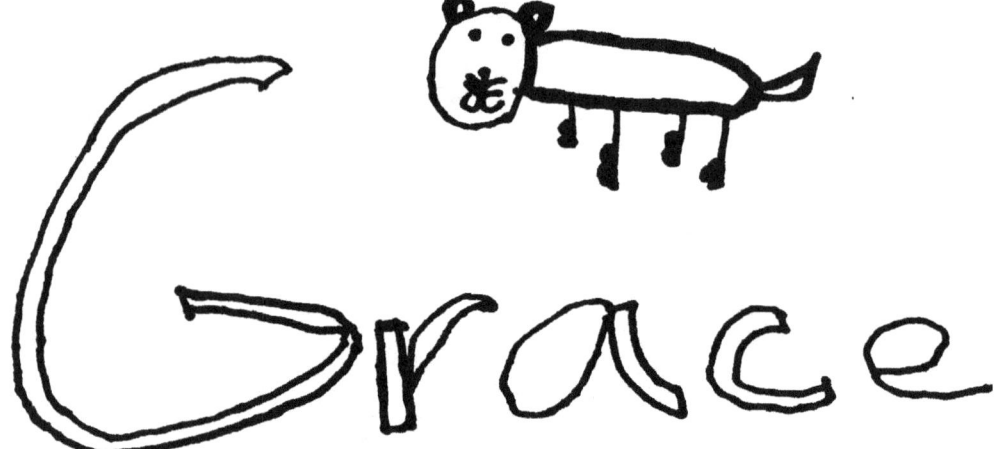

Creator Name: **Grace Hunt**

Age: **10**

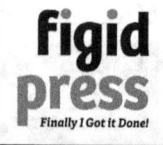

Cuddle Team Leader

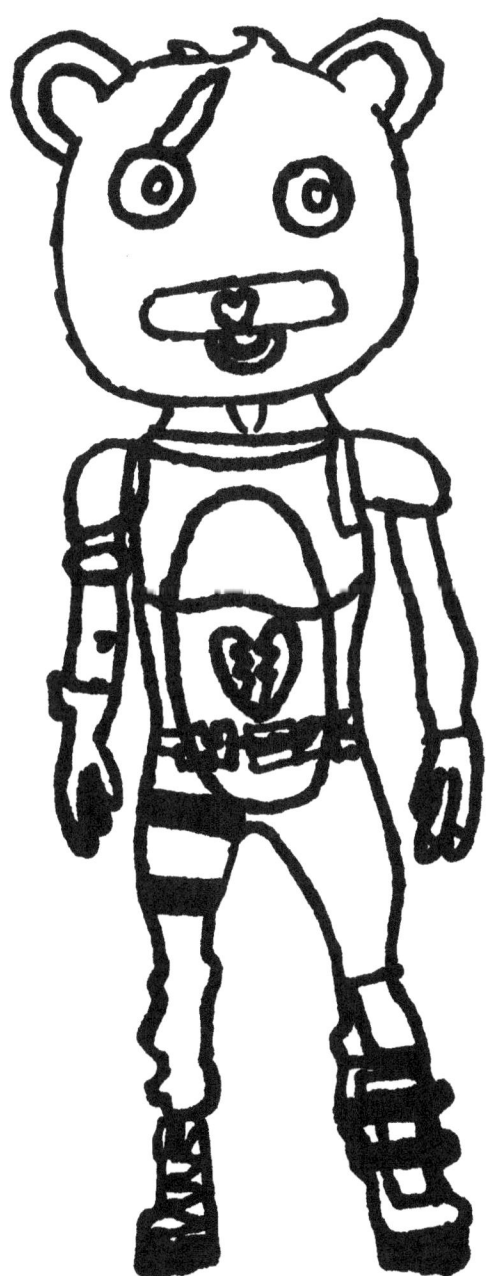

Creator Name:

Logan Stevenson

Age:

11

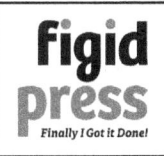

Footless Fred

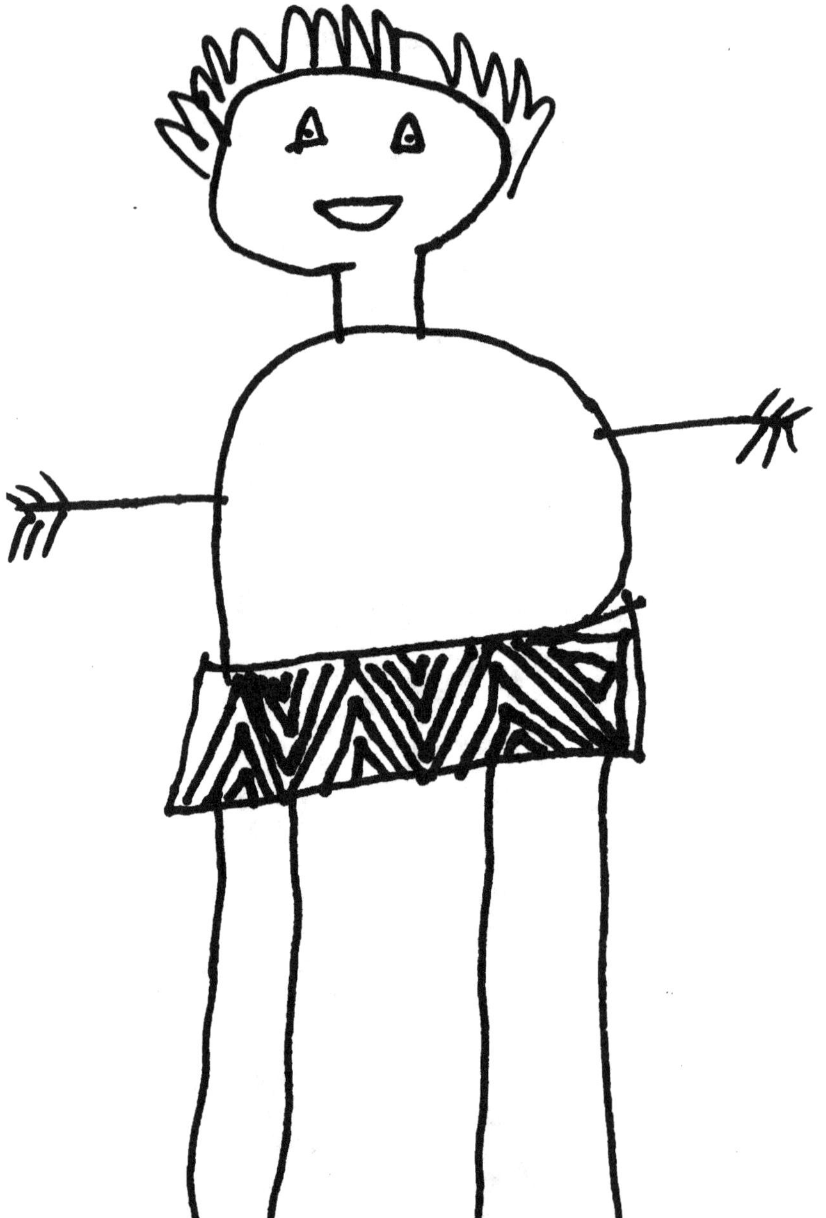

Creator Name: *Marcus Hyre*

Age: *11*

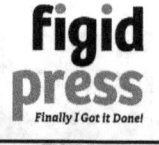

Homer Simpson

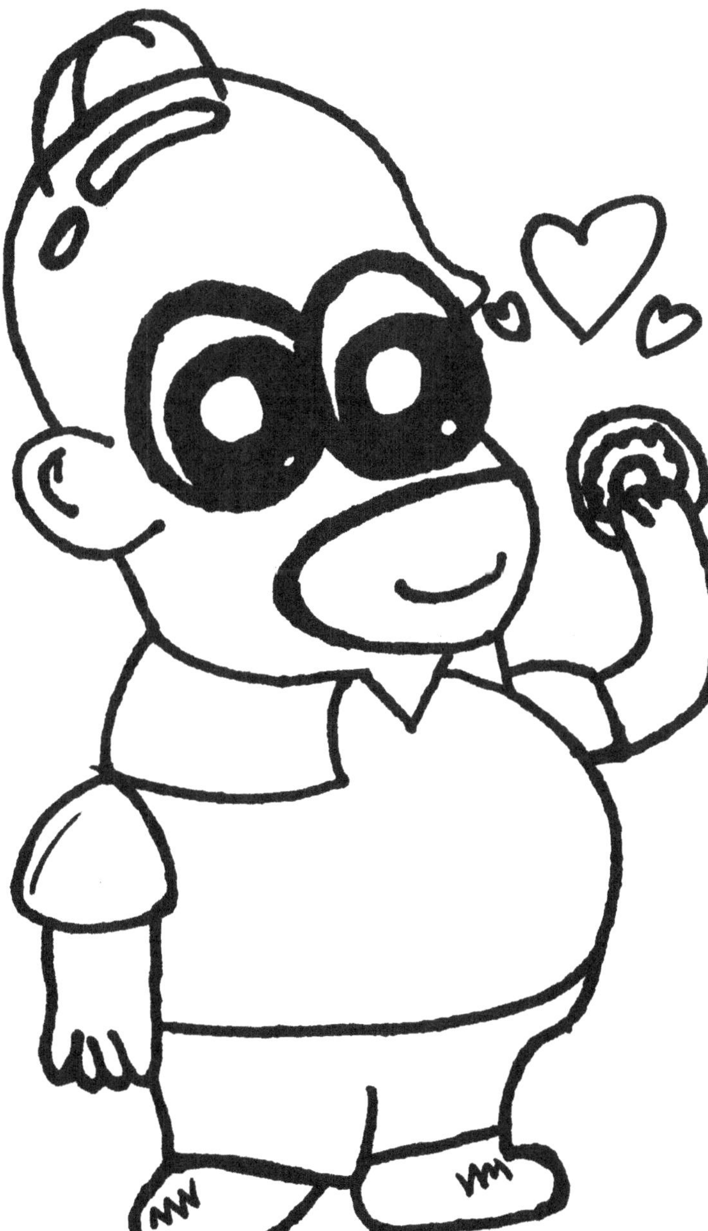

Creator Name:

Logan Stevenson

Age:

11

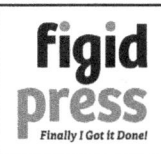

Jeff the Killer

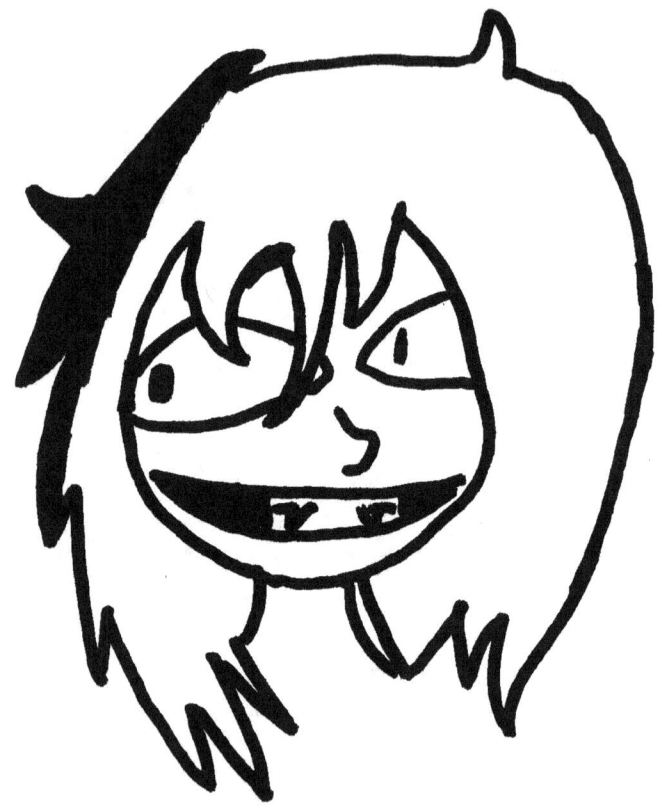

Creator Name: *Emilee Alderson*

Age: *11*

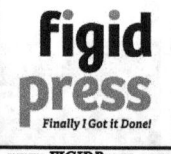

Mistris

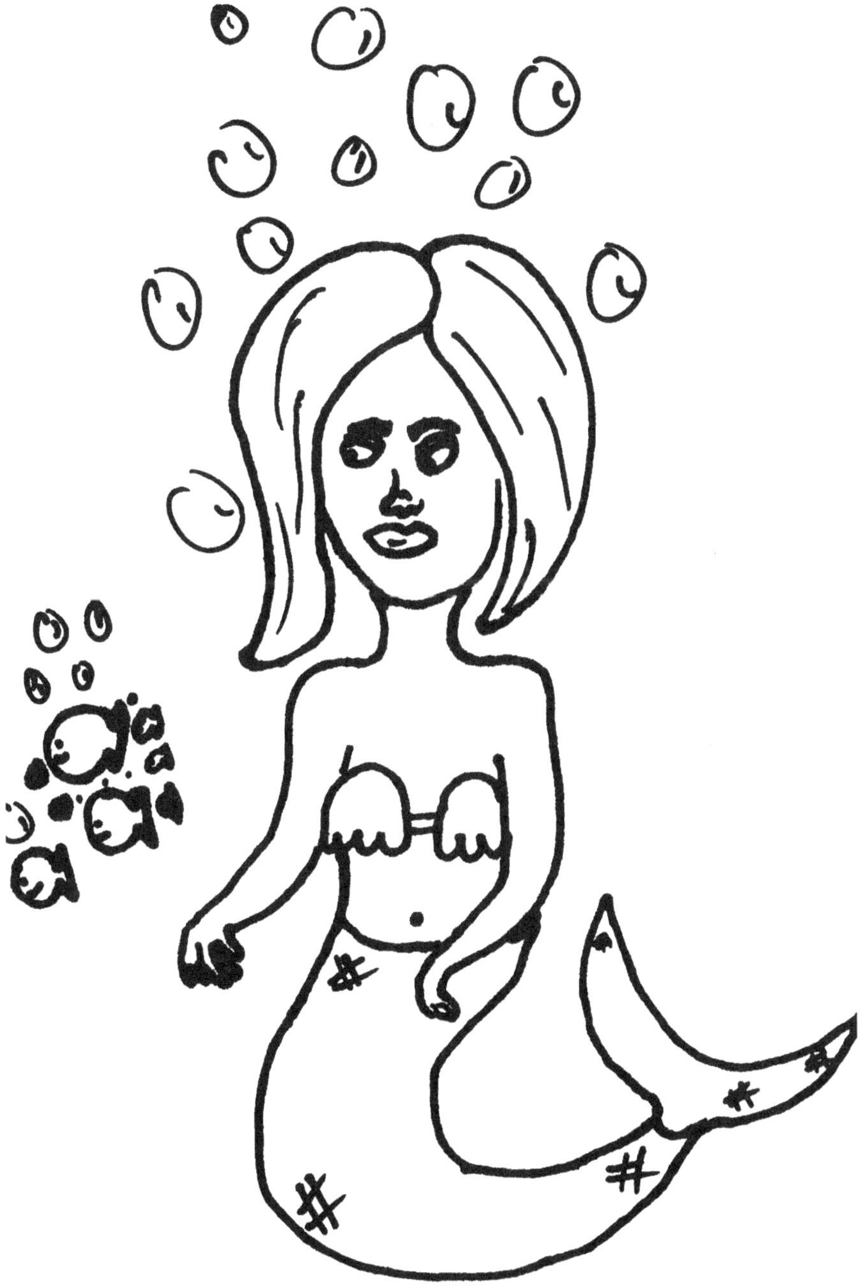

Creator Name: **Robyn Stevenson**

Age: **12**

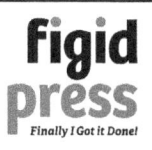

Nessie Boi

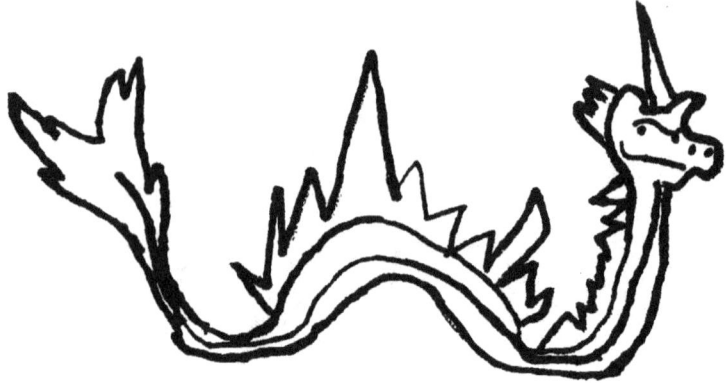

Creator Name: *Brayden Hunt*   Age: 13

Demono & Dogin

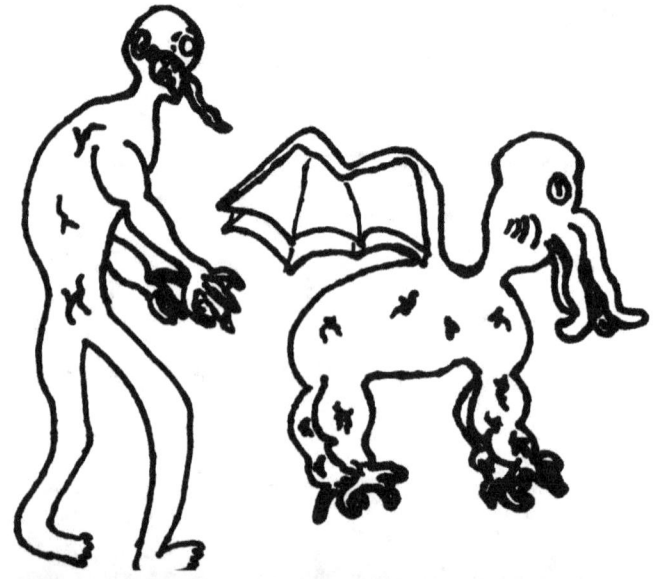

Creator Name: *Robyn Stevenson*   Age: 12

Mia

Creator Name: **Maleia**

Age: **14**

Del

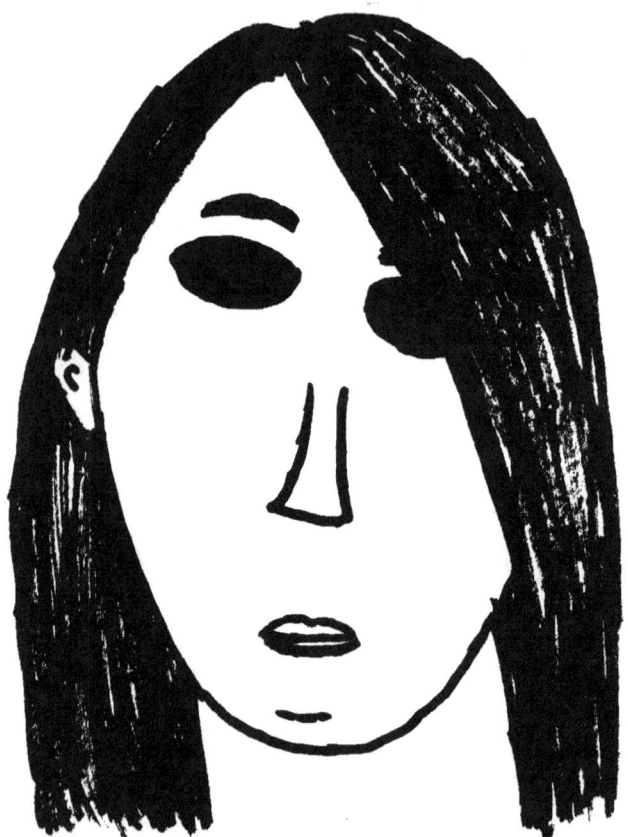

Creator Name: **Sara**

Age: **14**

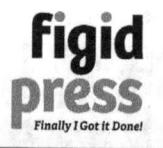

Eye

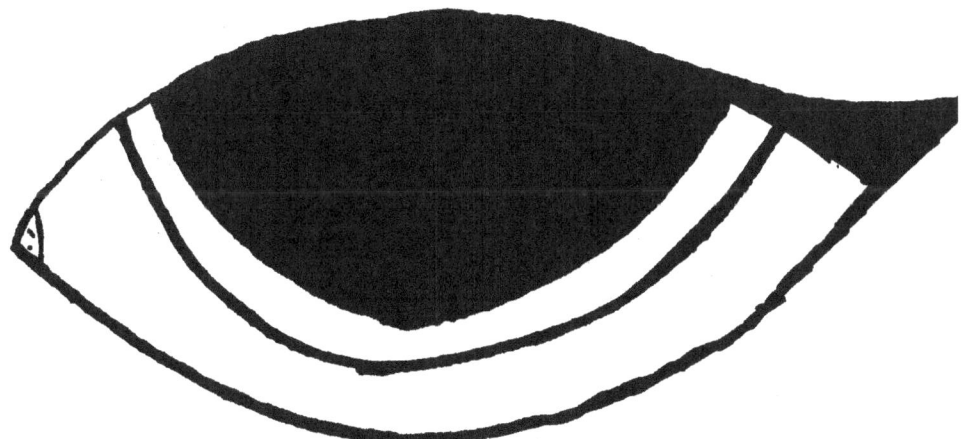

Creator Name: *Sara*

Age: **14**

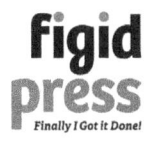

Eli Cipher

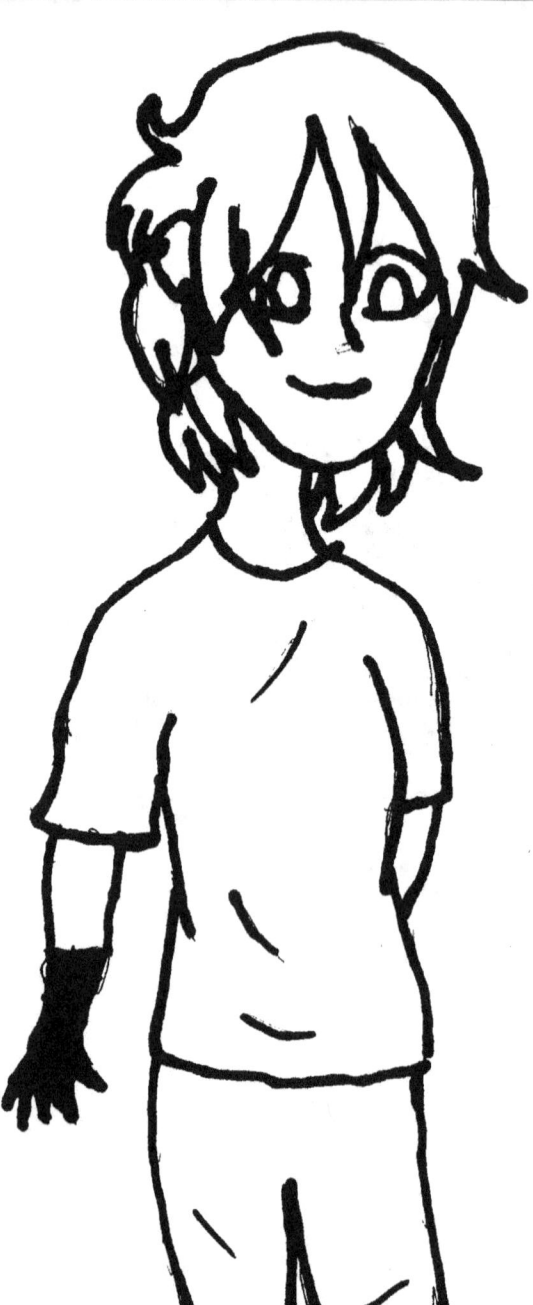

Creator Name: **Kaylee Vineyard**

Age: **14**

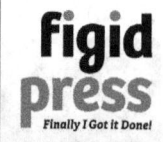

Keith from Voltron

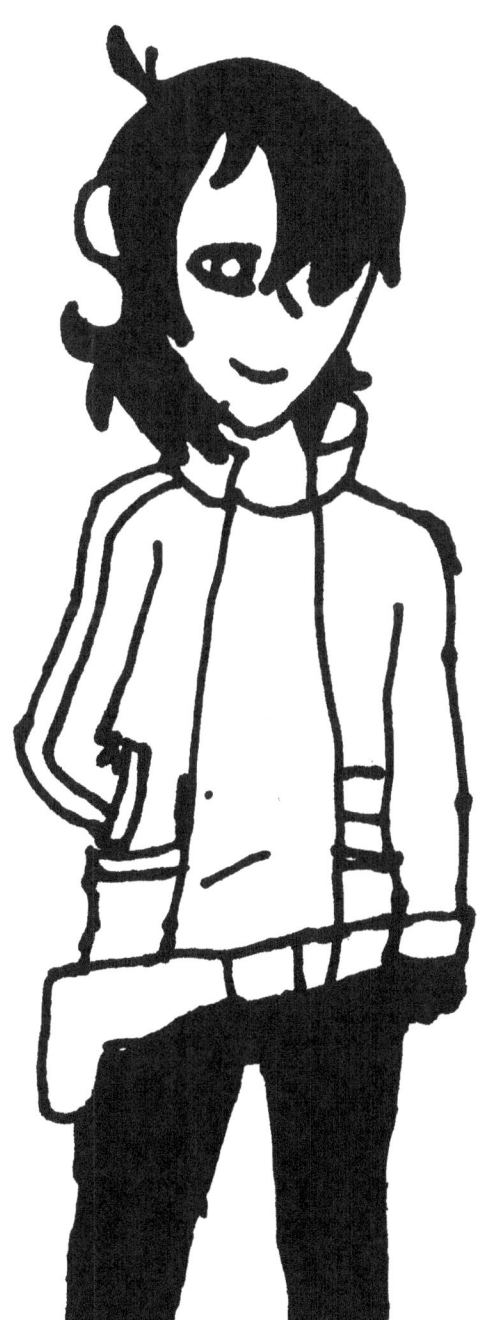

Creator Name: **Kaylee Vineyard**

Age: **14**

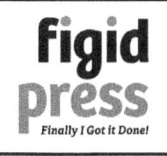

Will Cipher (Gravity Falls)

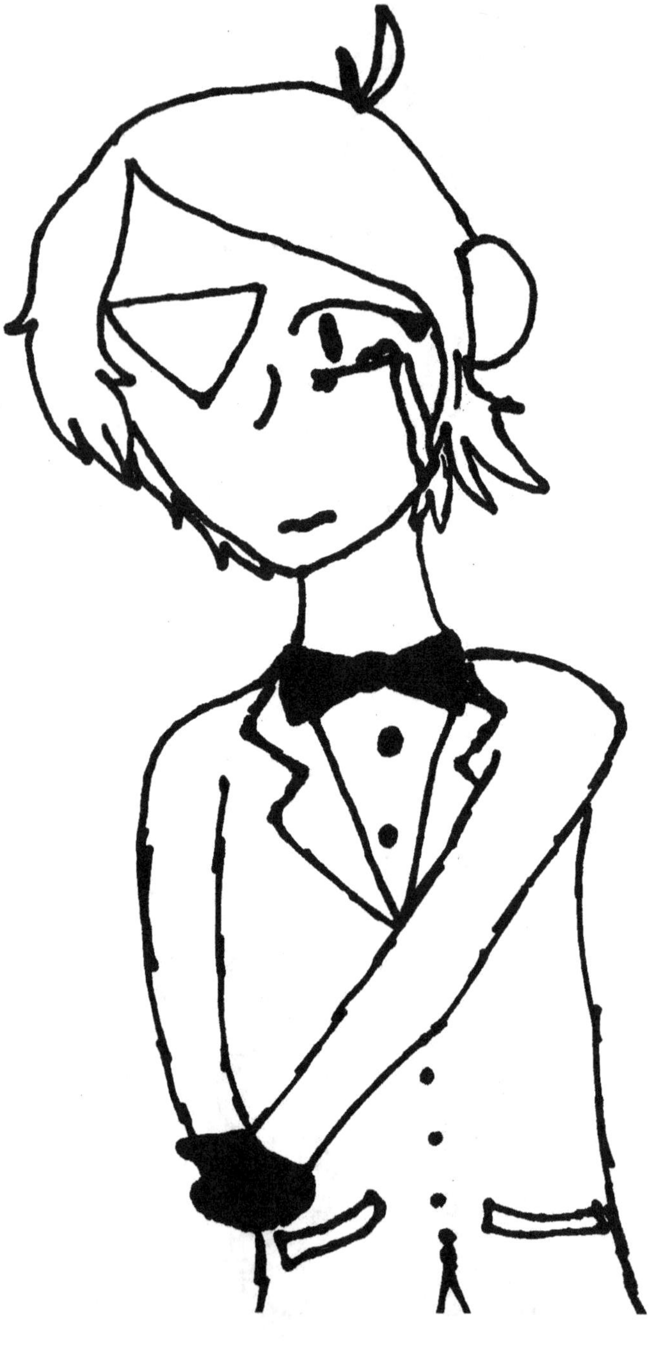

Creator Name: **Kaylee Vineyard**

Age: *14*

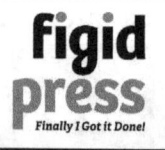

Rayman

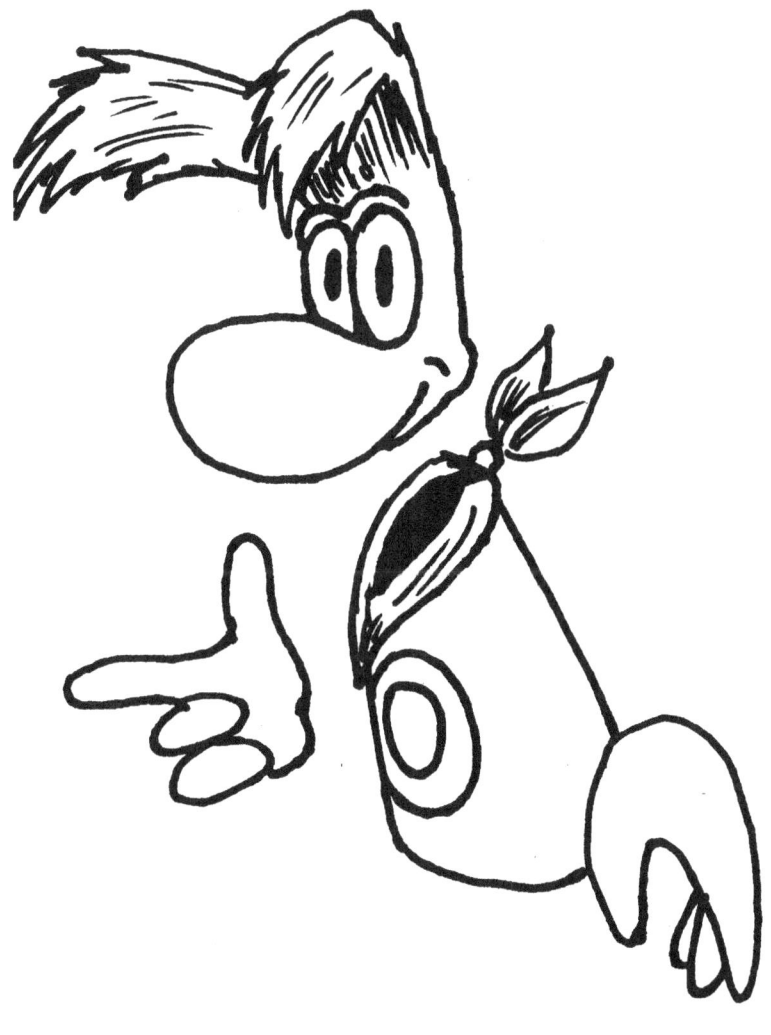

Creator Name: **Haley Jones**

Age: **15**

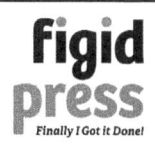

www.FIGIDPress.com

Brook

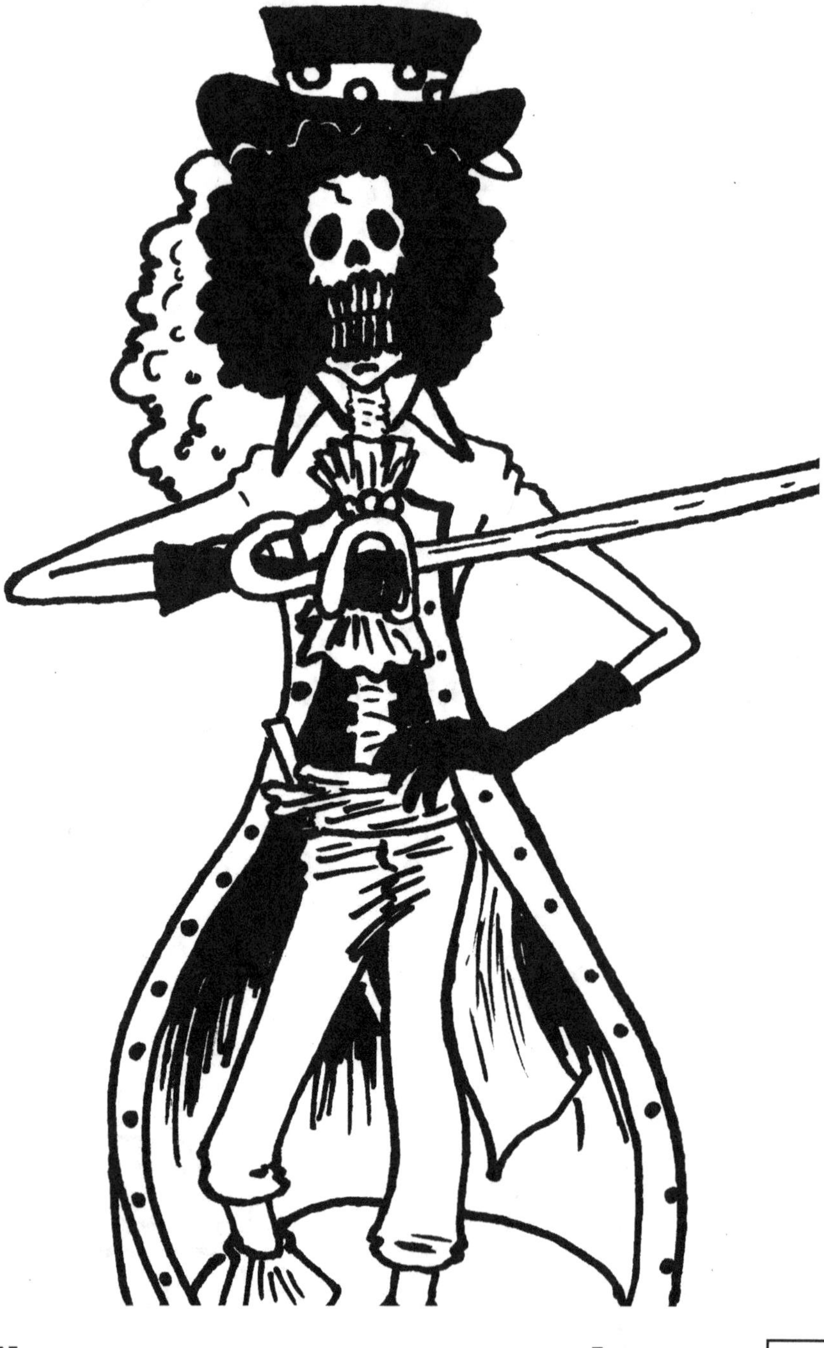

Creator Name:
Haley Jones

Age:
15

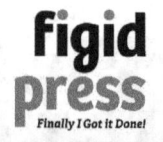

Snufkin

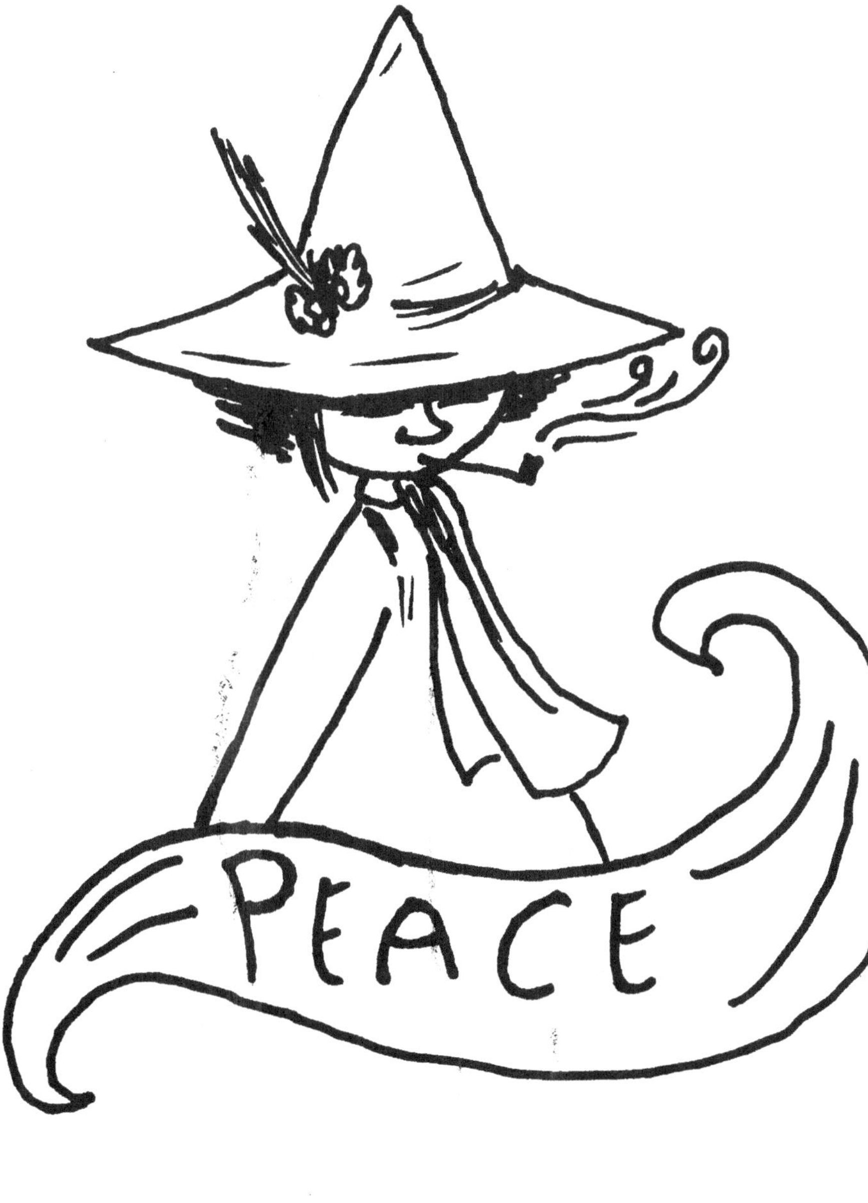

PEACE

Creator Name: **Haley Jones**

Age: **15**

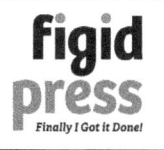

Ghostface

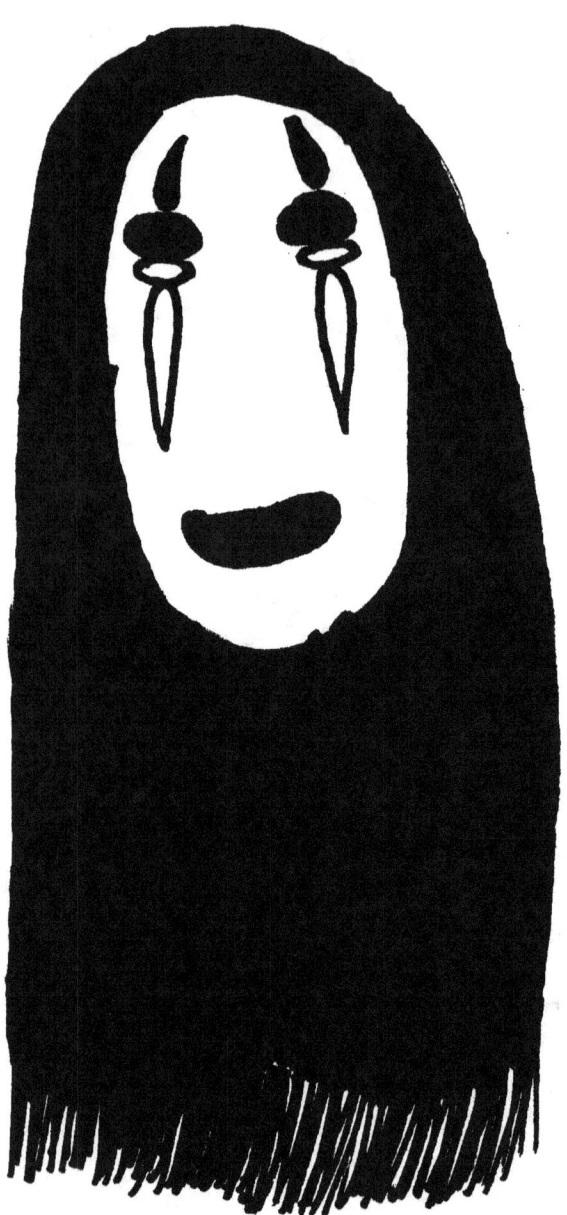

Creator Name: **Kristi Davidson**

Age: **15**

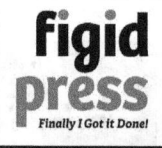

Bendy

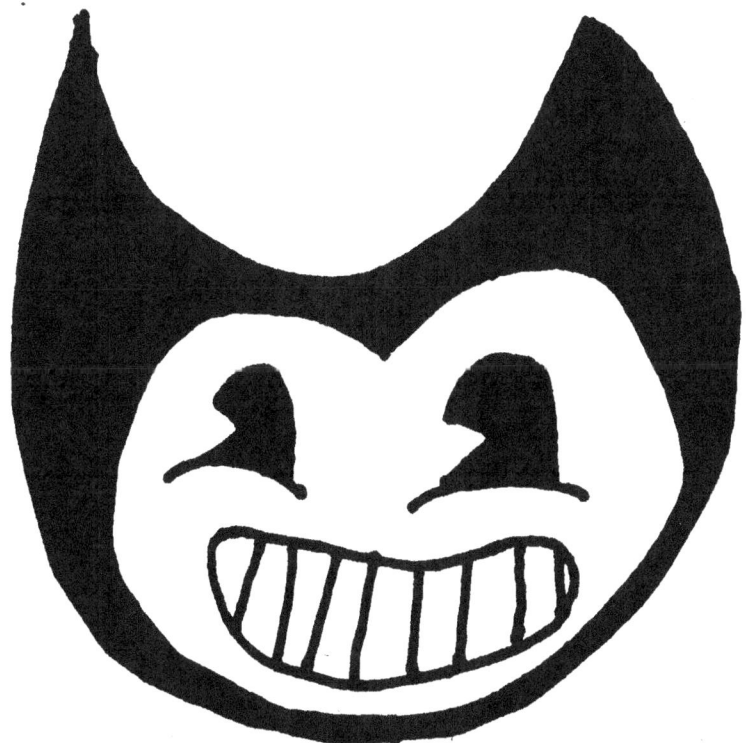

Creator Name: **Kristi Davidson**

Age: **15**

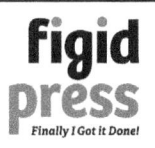

Mouse of Omnipotence

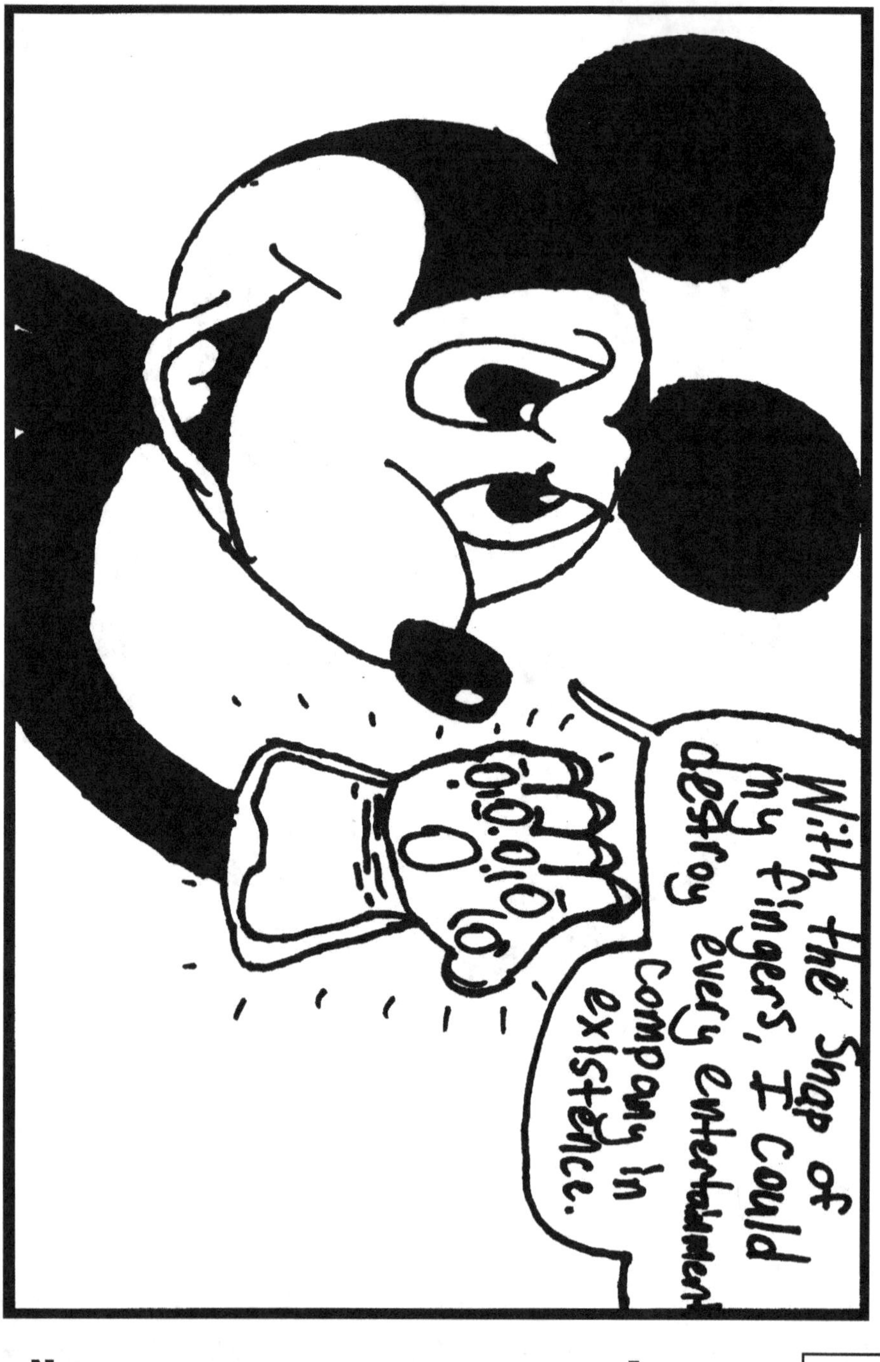

> With the snap of my fingers, I could destroy every entertainment company in existence.

Creator Name: **Bailey Hartrich**

Age: **16**

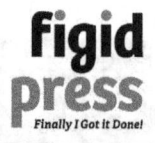

Jack Jack

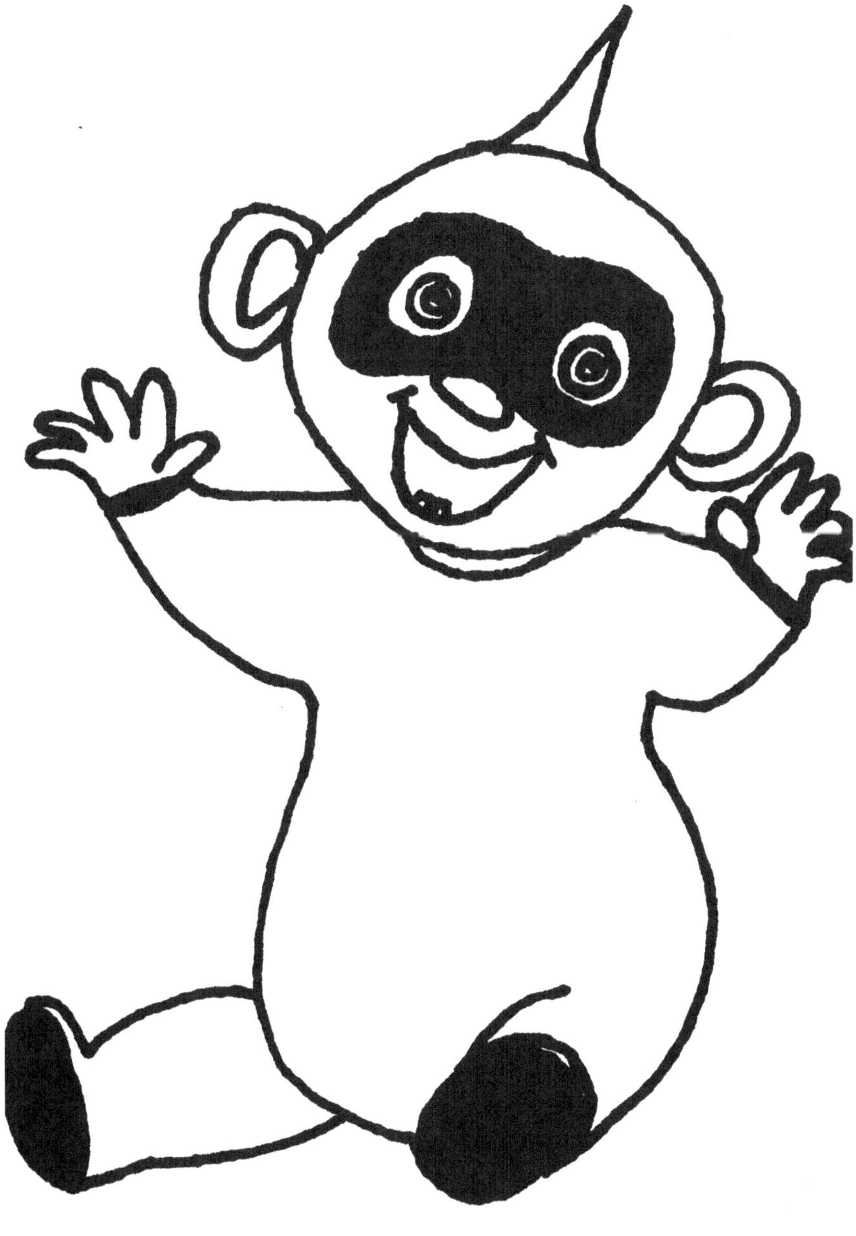

Creator Name: **Lacey Shaw**

Age: **17**

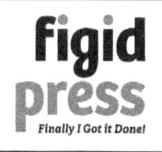

Domino

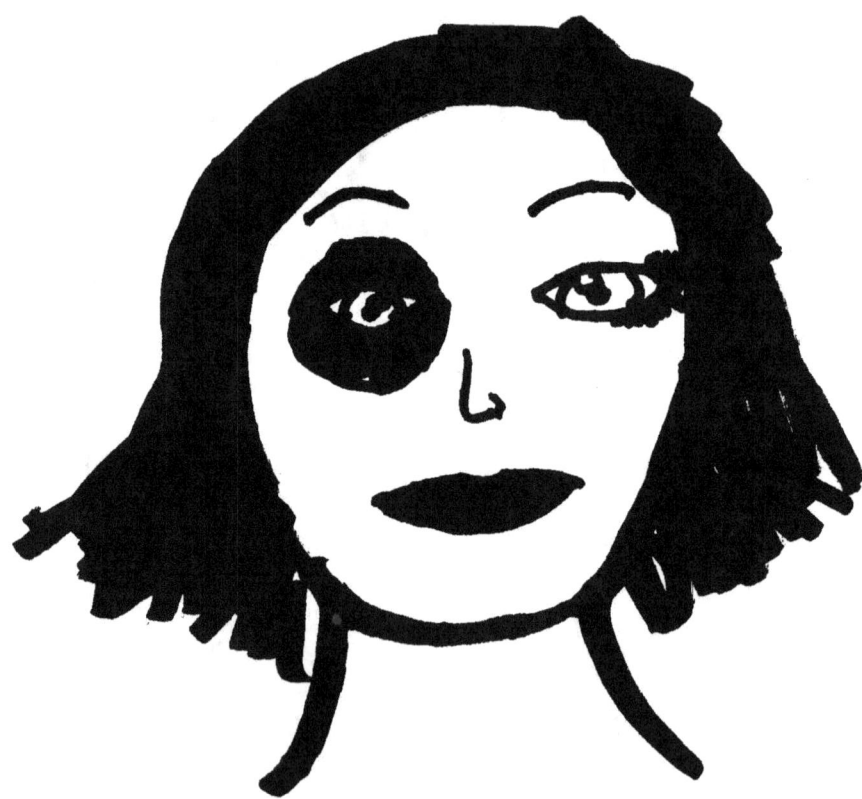

Creator Name: **Sydney Green**

Age: **17**

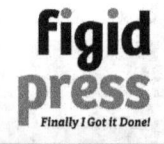
www.FIGIDPress.com

Pebbles Flintstone

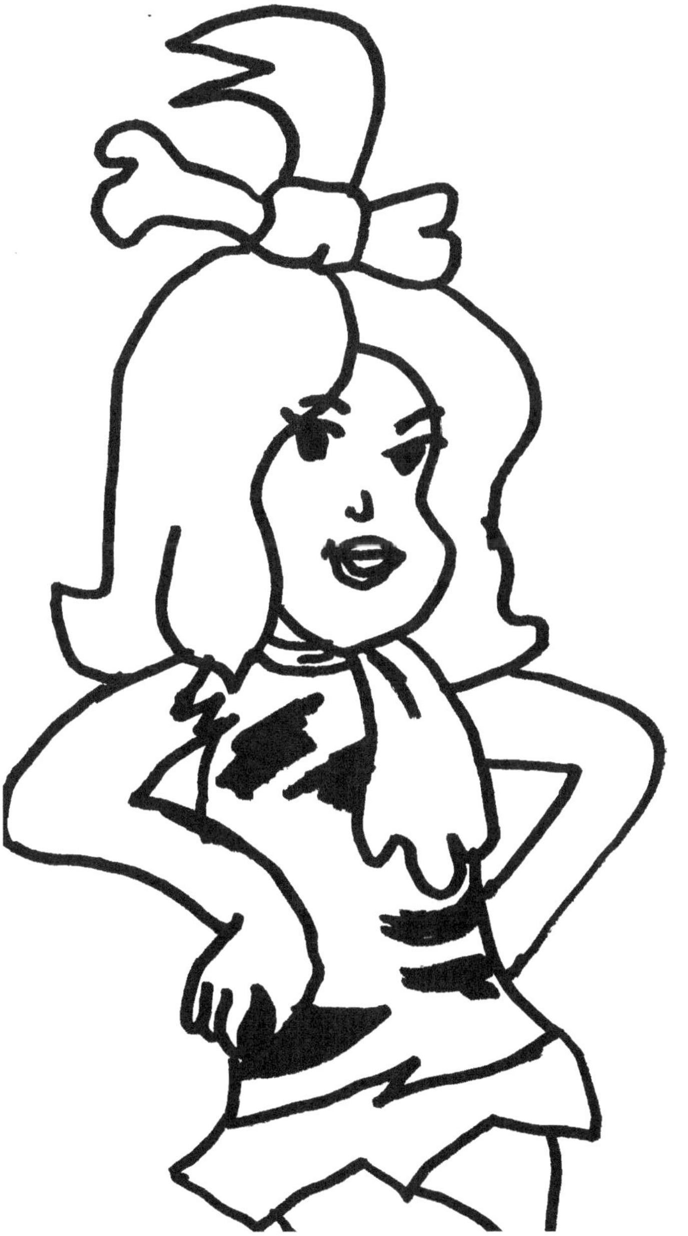

Creator Name: *Sydney Green*

Age: *17*

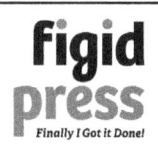

Runner No. 6

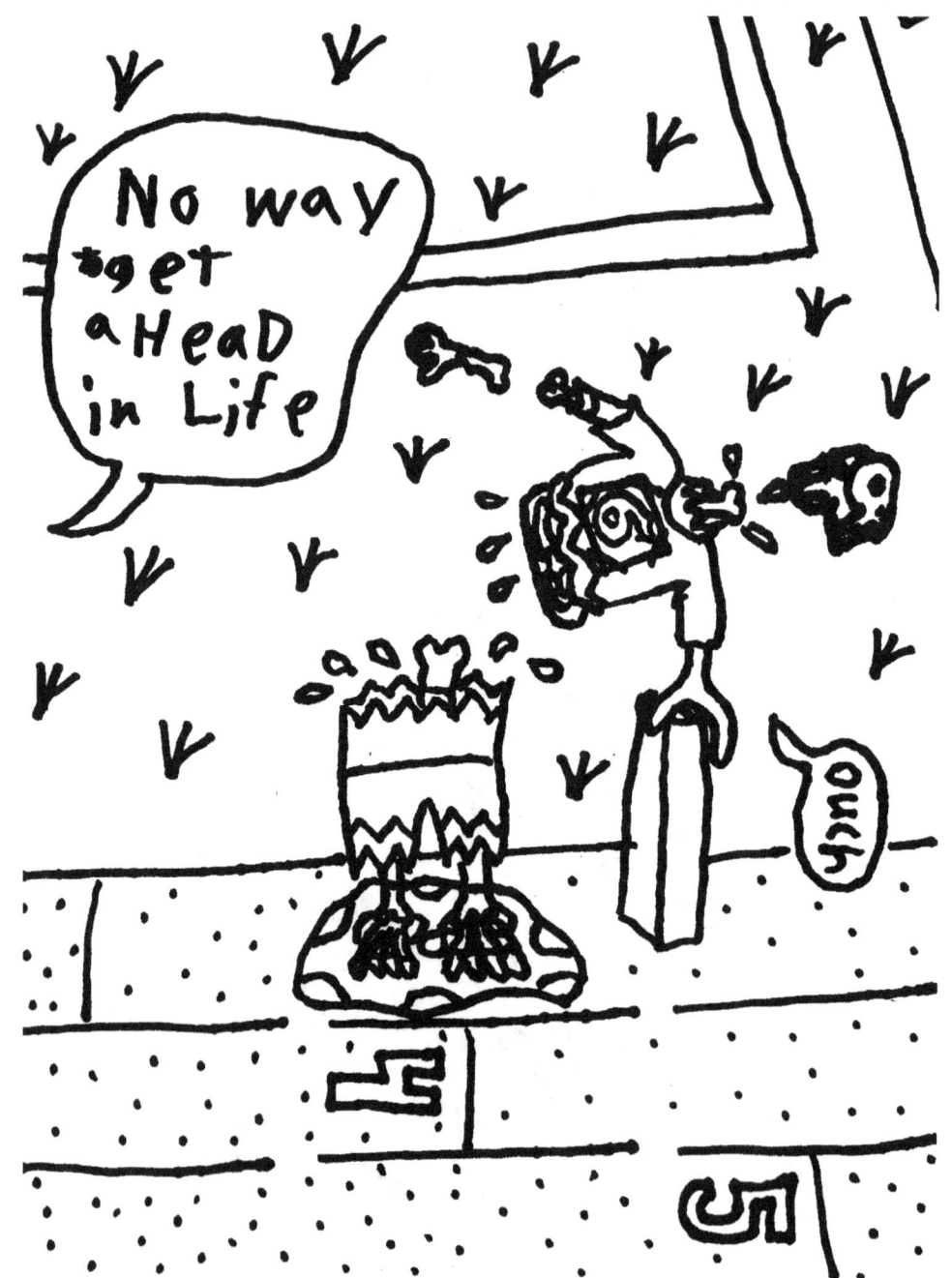

Creator Name: **Travis Standridge**

Age: 17

Lilyan

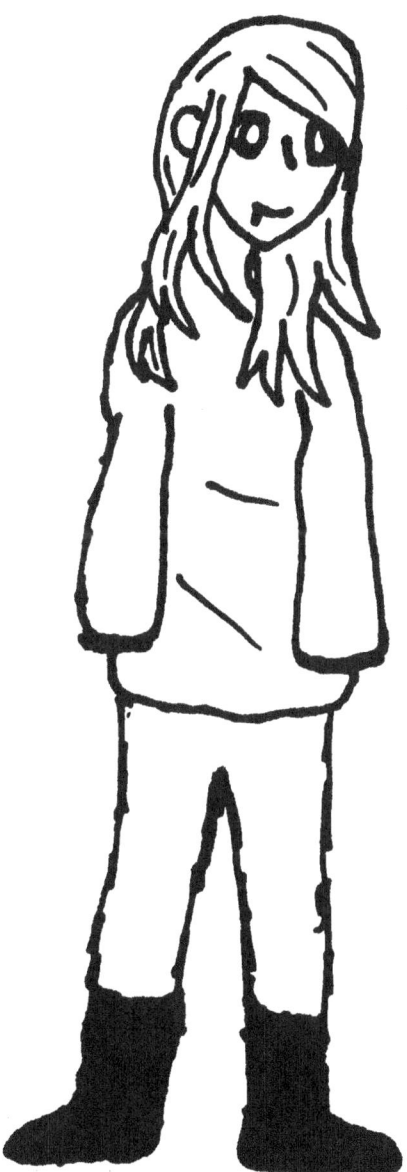

Creator Name: **Kaylee**

Age: *17*

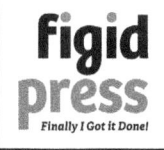

Iphigenia

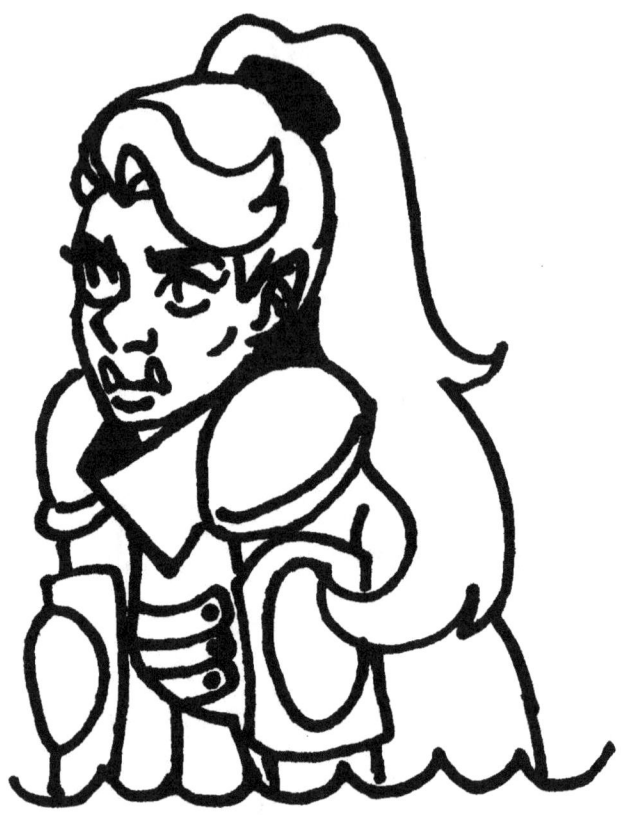

Creator Name: **Miranda Britton**

Age: 20

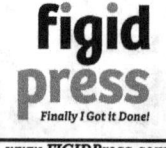

Rowlet

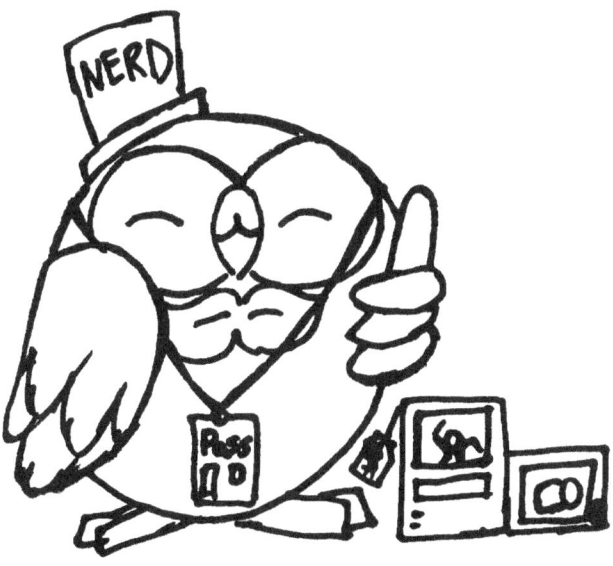

Creator Name: **Renessa Jones** Age: **22**

Mimikyu

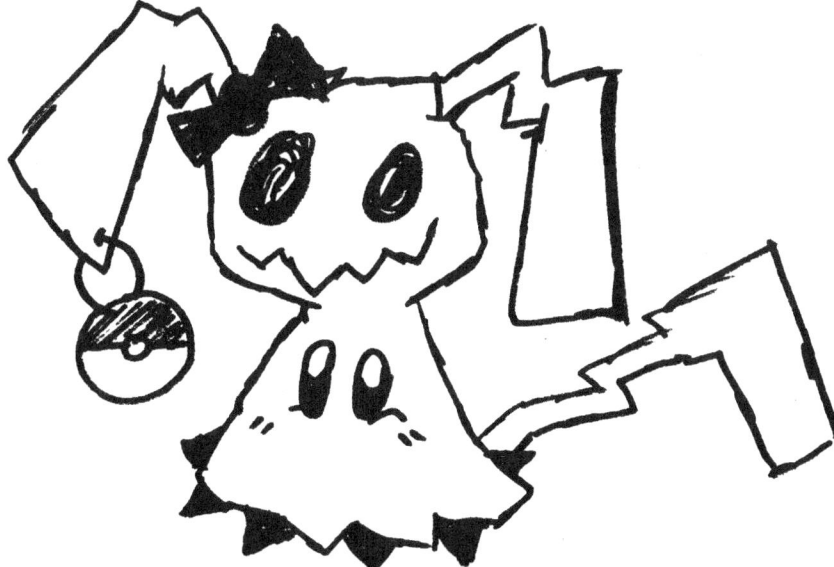

Creator Name: **Renessa Jones** Age: **22**

Verrin

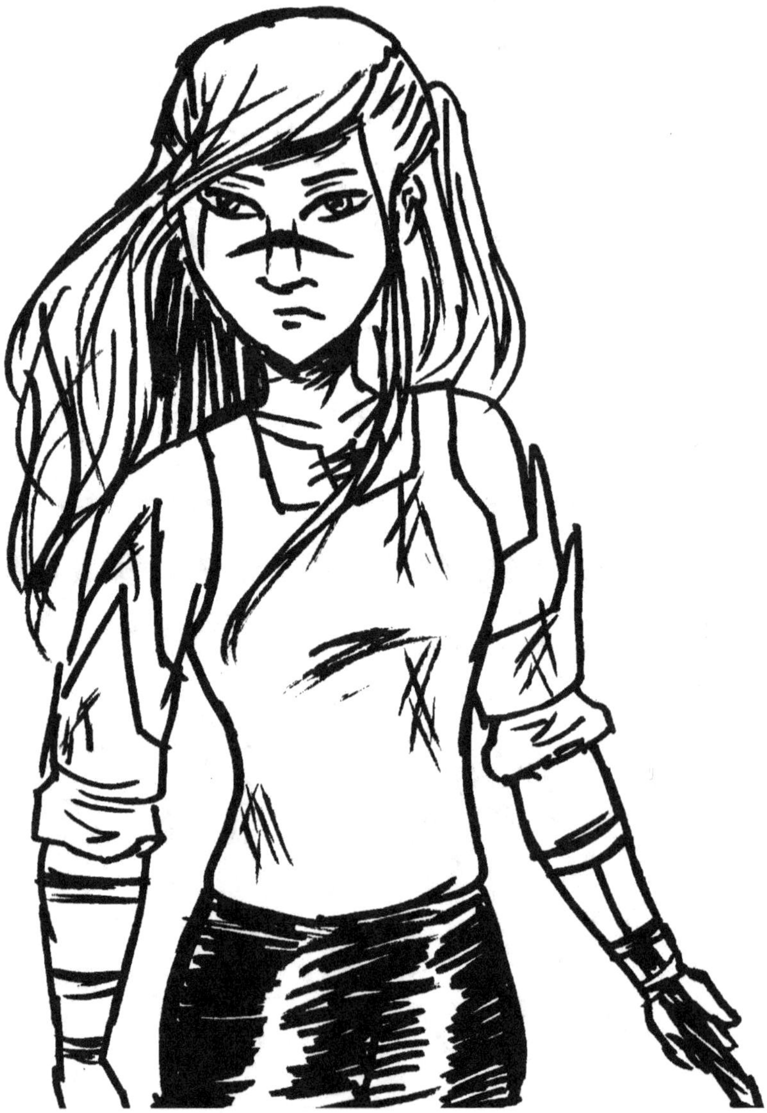

Creator Name: **Beth**

Age: *25*

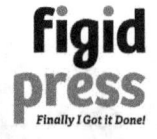

Lucy Mutters

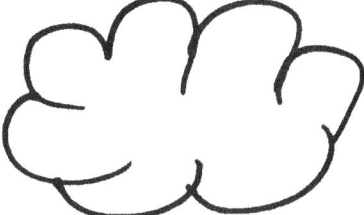
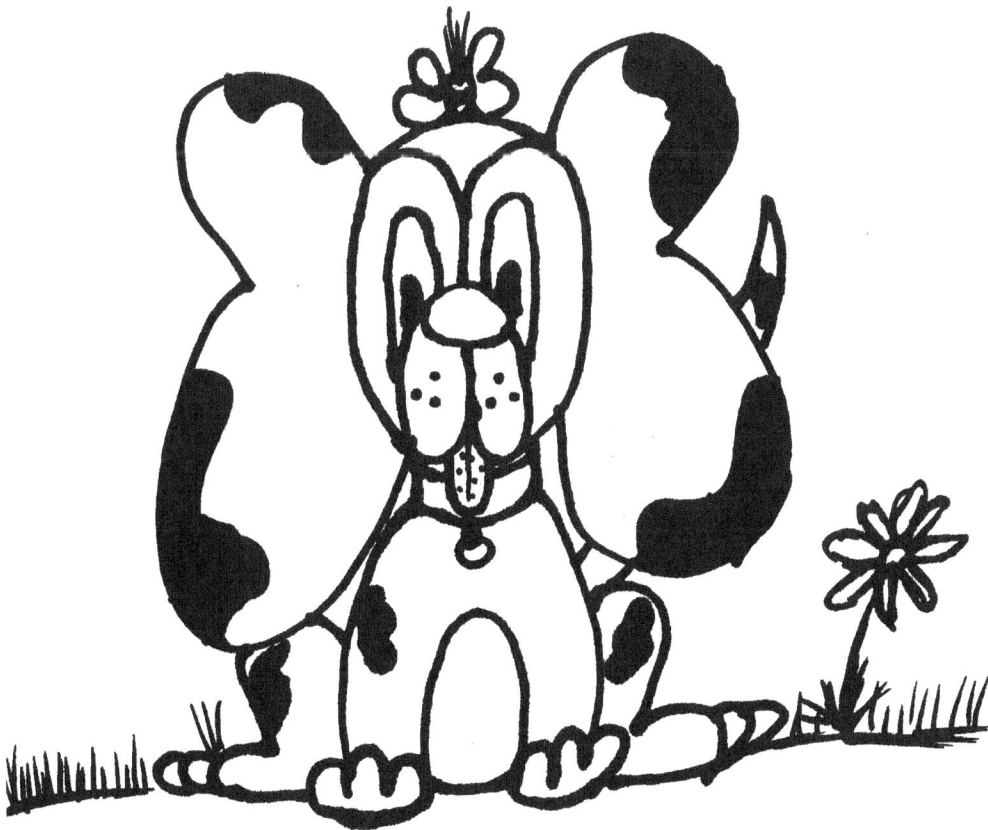

Creator Name: **Nicole Stevenson**

Age: **31**

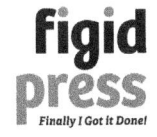

Not One Punch Man

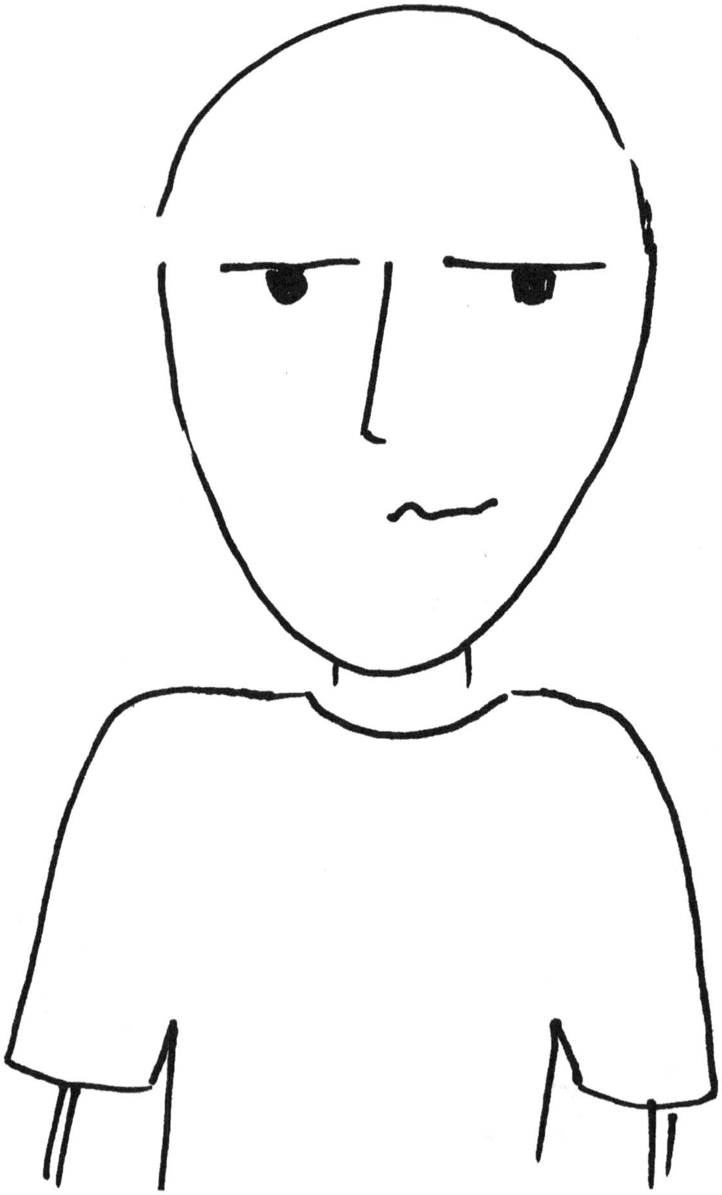

Creator Name:

William Brasley

Age:

32

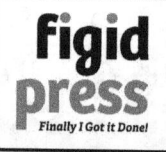

Darth Garfield

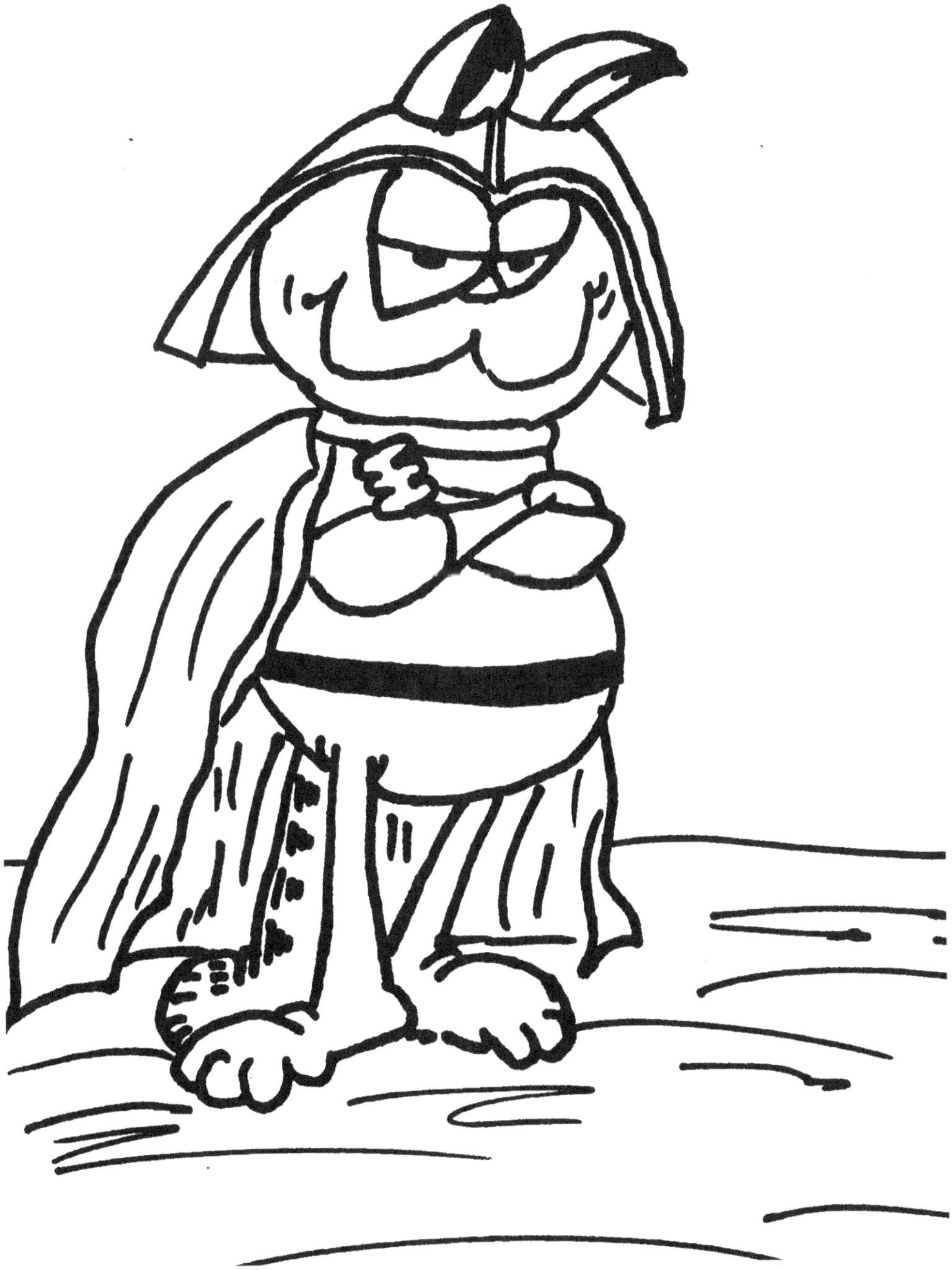

Creator Name: **Bethany Dunlap**

Age: **32**

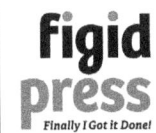

Commissioner Davis

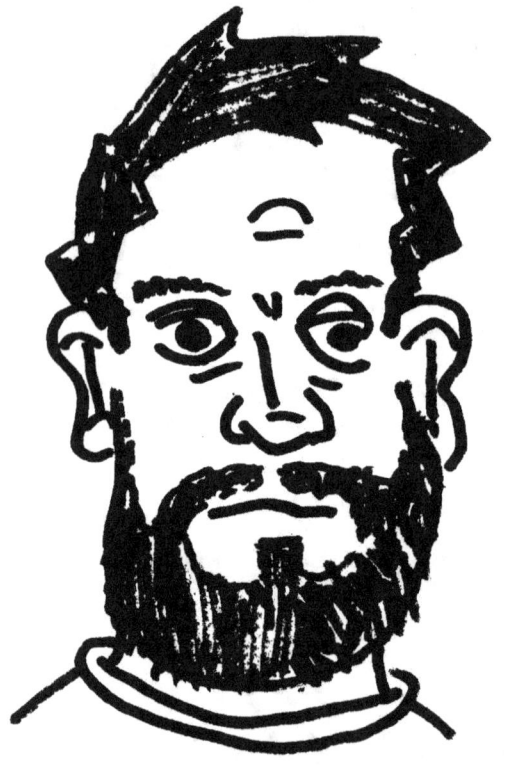

"Commissioner Davis"

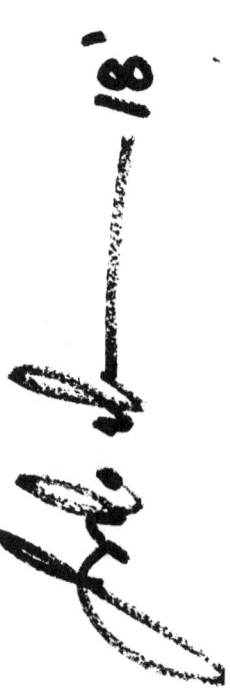

Creator Name: *Joe D. Davis*

Age:

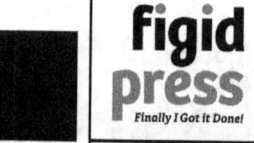

Umbrellian

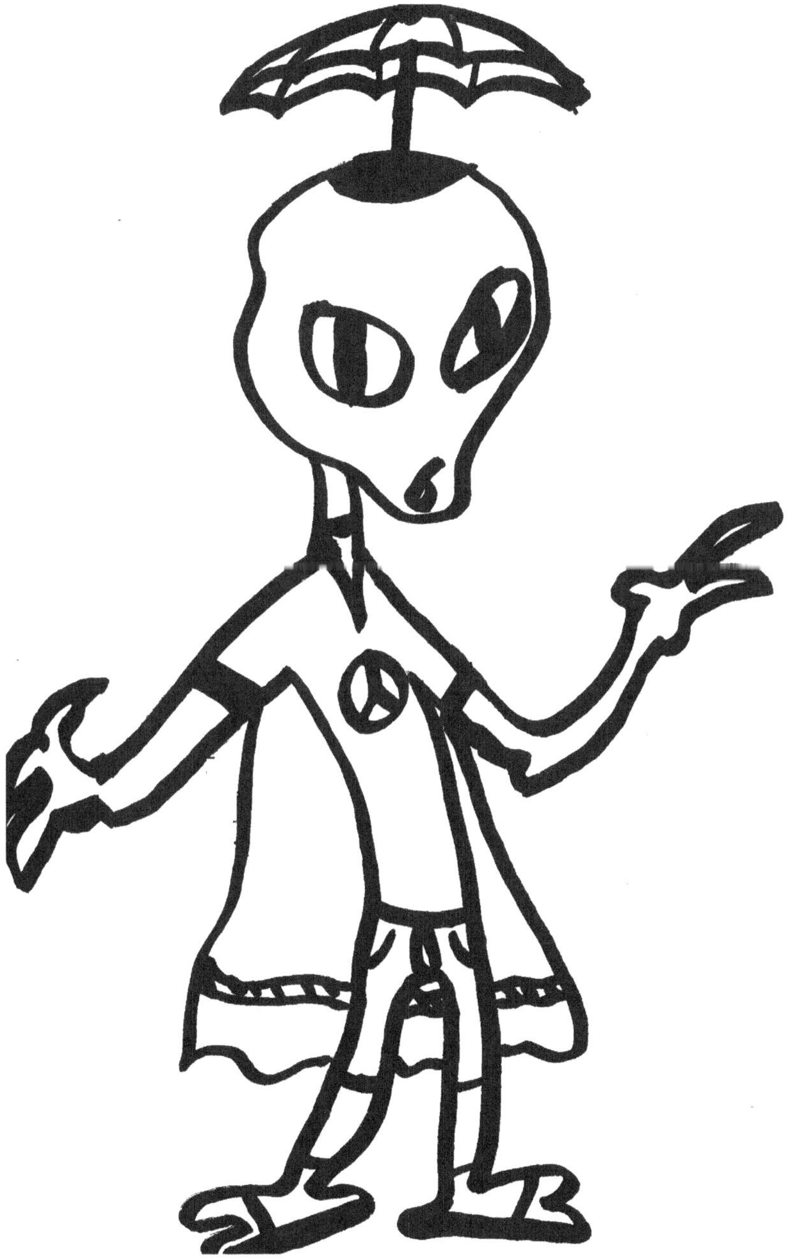

Creator Name: **Kevin E.**

Age: **34**

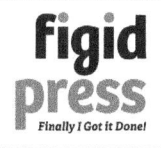

Special Edd

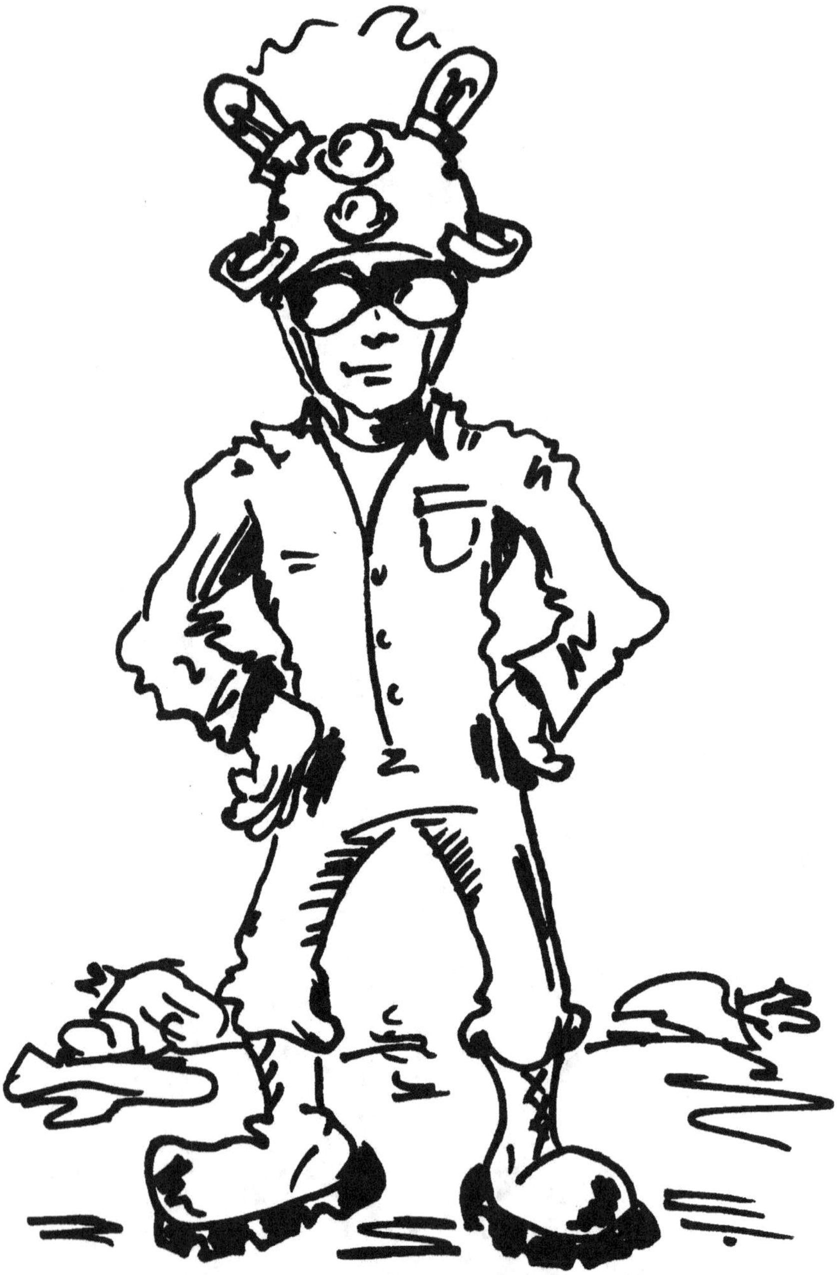

Creator Name: **Gary Stevenson**

Age: 39

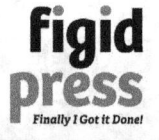

Corporal Pig

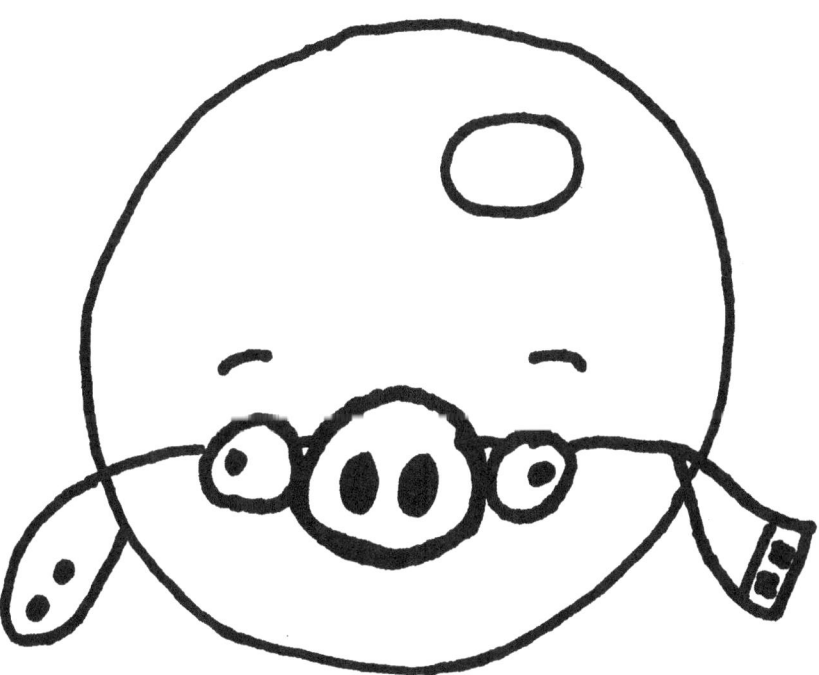

Creator Name: **Diana**

Age: **41**

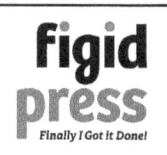

Flyguy

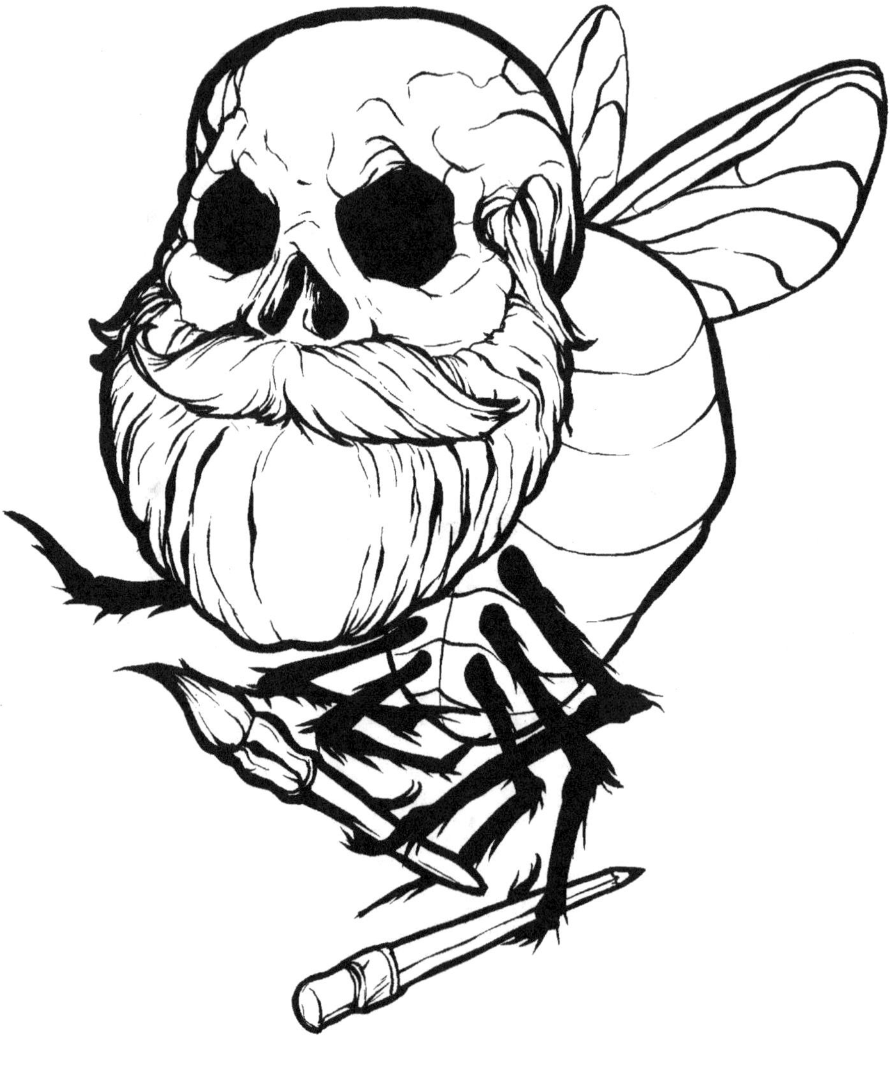

Creator Name: James Thiry

Age: 100

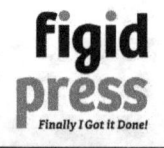

Macho Muchacho

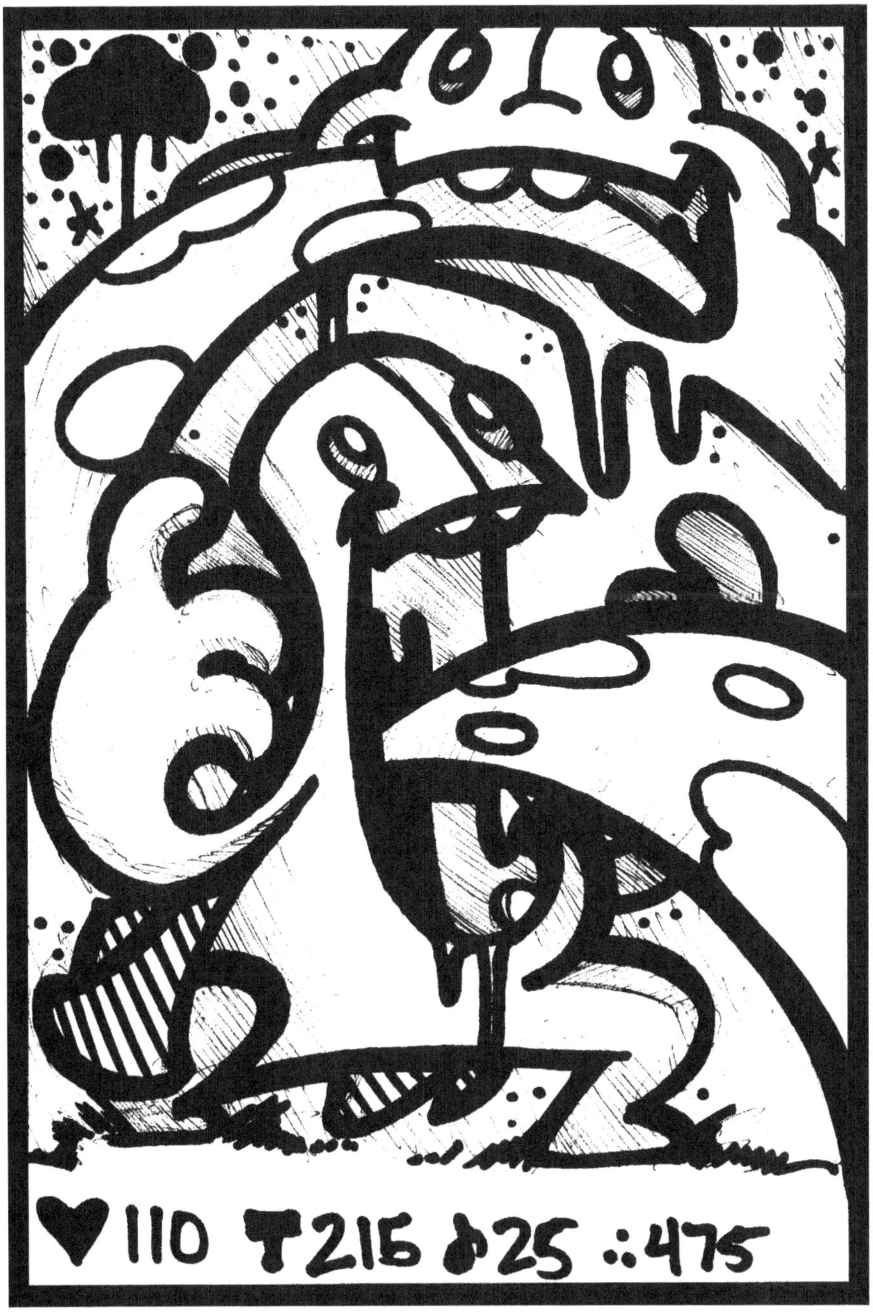

♥ 110 ♆ 215 ♪ 25 ∴ 475

Creator Name: **KLWDS**

Age: **100**

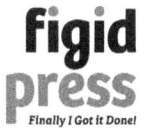

Super Olive

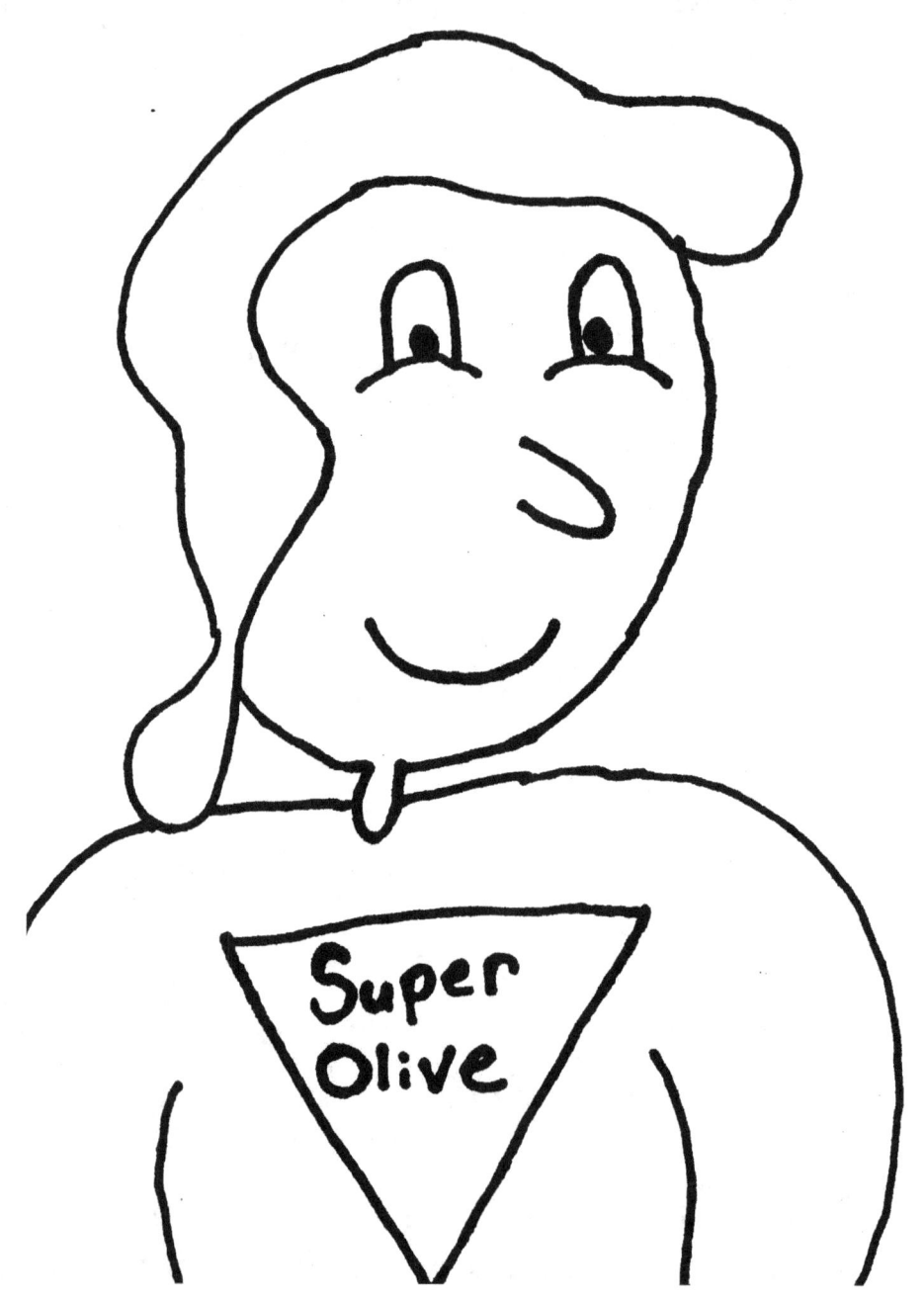

Creator Name: **Sam Hyre**

Age: **Dad**

figid press
Finally I Got it Done!
www.FIGIDPress.com

My Convention Experience

Use the following pages to record your experiences, thoughts, and things you did at the show. You had a great time and saw so many cool things, so don't forget them. Take a few minutes and record them for yourself and future generations.

My Convention experience

How did I get to the show?

_____

Here's some cool things that happened.

_____

_____

_____

_____

_____

_____

_____

_____

Things I need to do when I come back.

_____

_____

_____

_____

_____

My Convention Experience (Continued)

Panels I attended!

_____
_____
_____
_____
_____

People I met!

_____
_____
_____
_____
_____

Vendor booths to visit again next year!

_____
_____
_____
_____
_____
_____

My brush with greatness.

Getting to meet: _____

Item I had autographed: _____

Did I get a picture?   Yes   No

Here's what happened:

_____
_____
_____
_____
_____
_____
_____
_____
_____
_____
_____
_____
_____
_____

My Convention Story

These are my experiences at the convention over the weekend.

My Convention Story

These are my experiences at the convention over the weekend.

My Convention Story

These are my experiences at the convention over the weekend.

More Character Creation ahead!

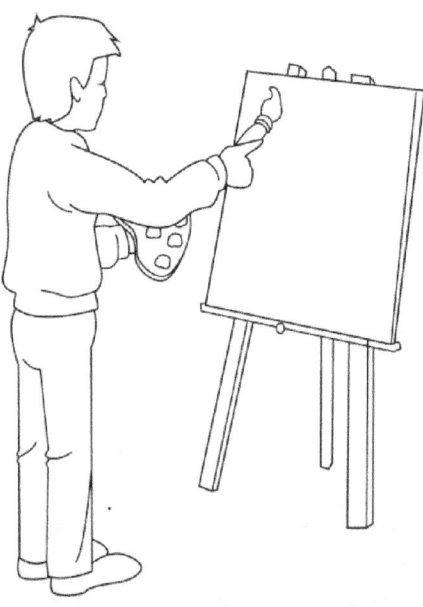

Amazing Characters

Your First Name:

Your Last Name:

Age:

Character Name:

Special Powers:

Weakness / Vulnerbilities:

Origin or Background story:

Draw your character in a new pose!

Sketch a team of characters here!

Make your own comic pages.

The following pages are blank versions of different comic pages. Make copies to practice showing your character in story form.

If you fill these pages up with different stories, then contact John at FIGIDPress@Gmail.com and he'll send you PDF template pages that you can print out to make more.

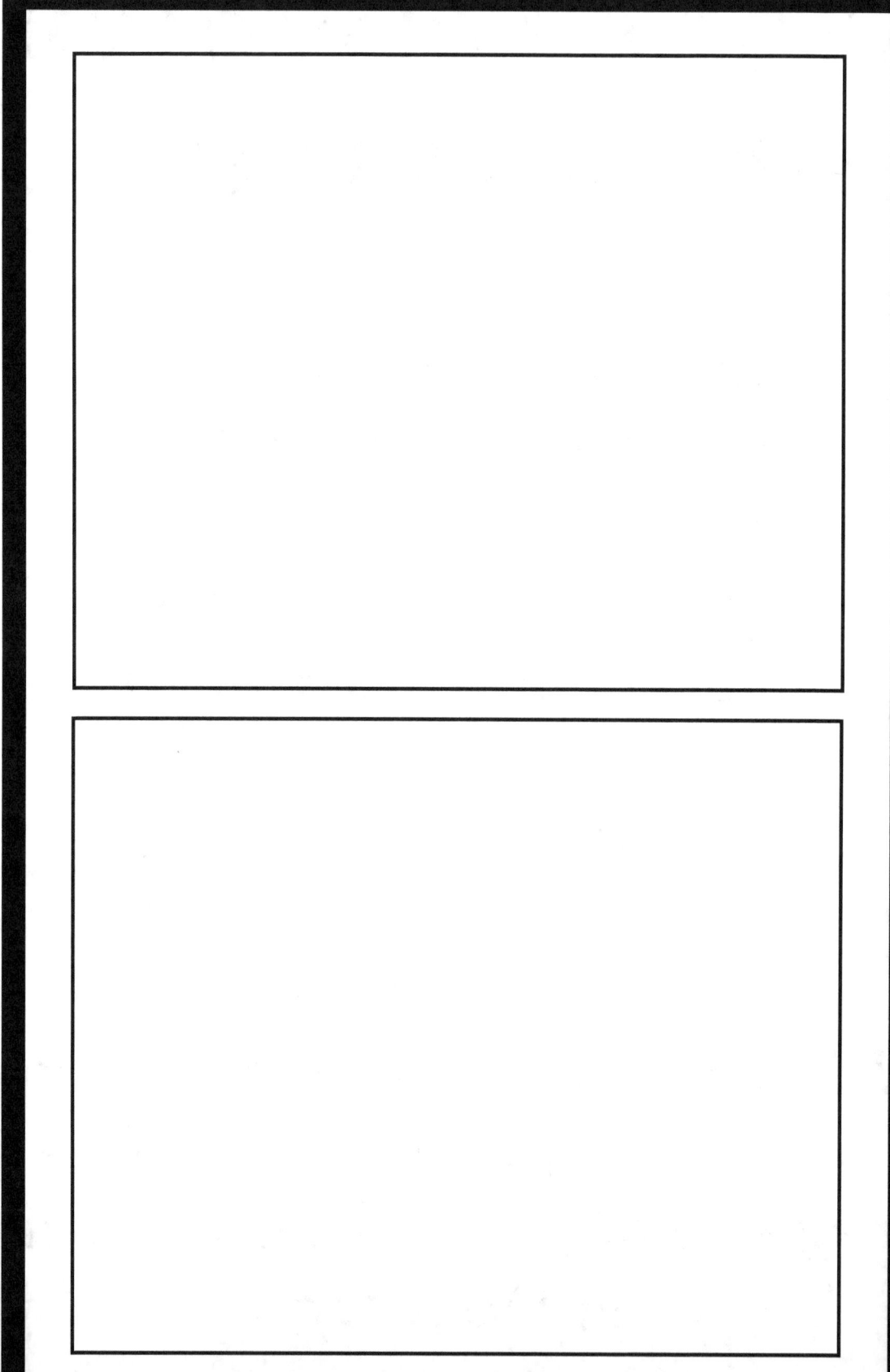

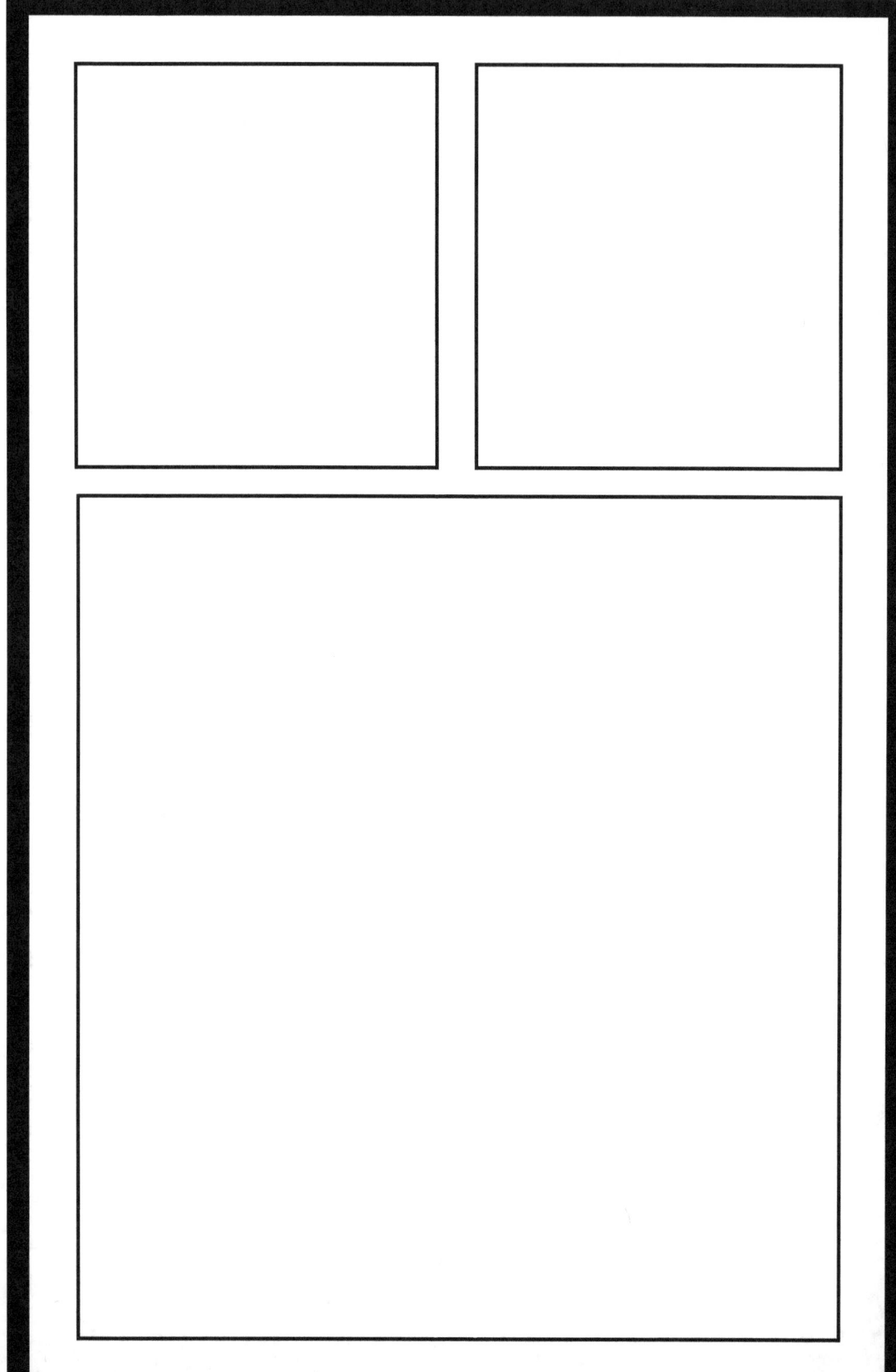

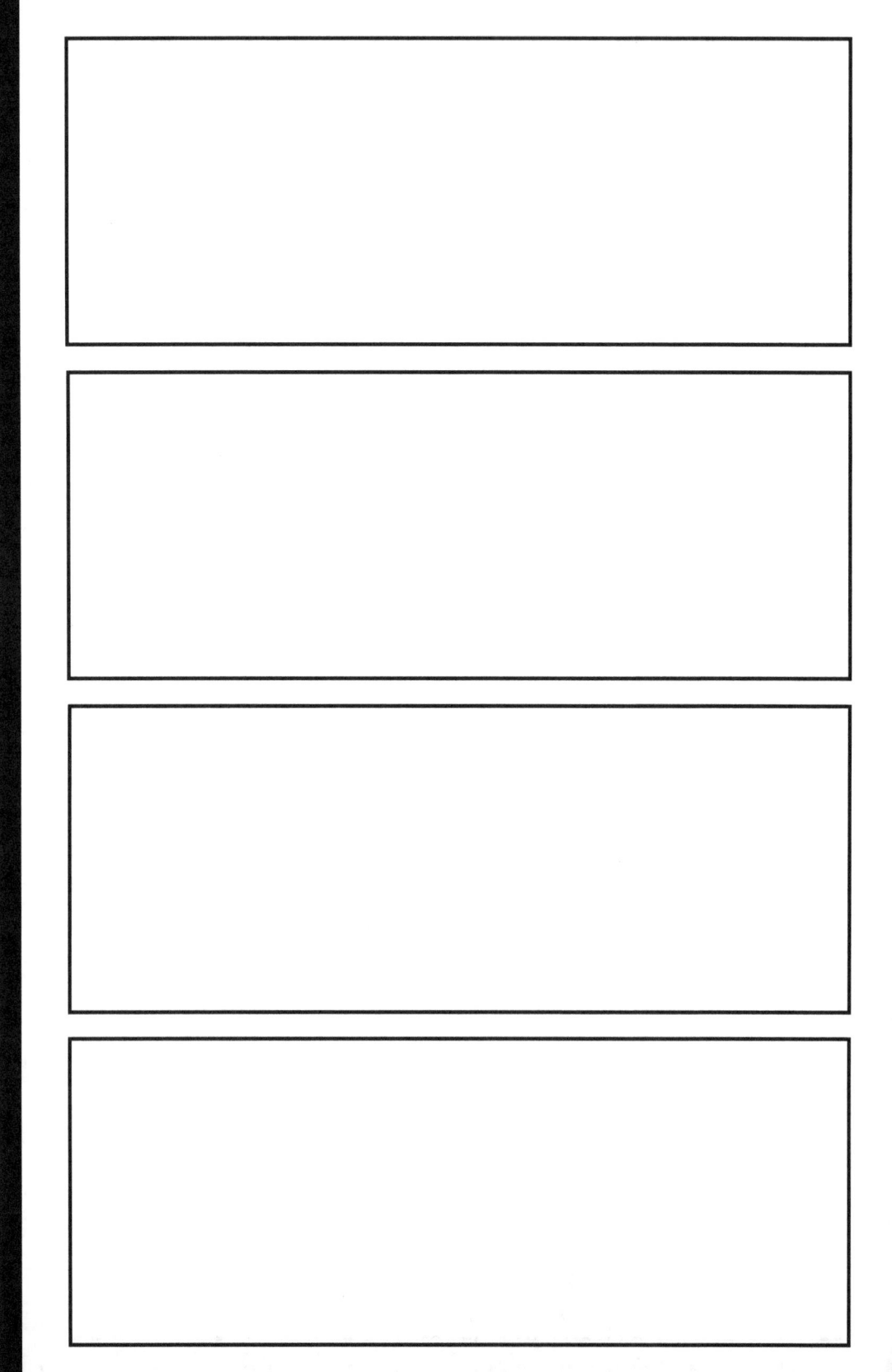

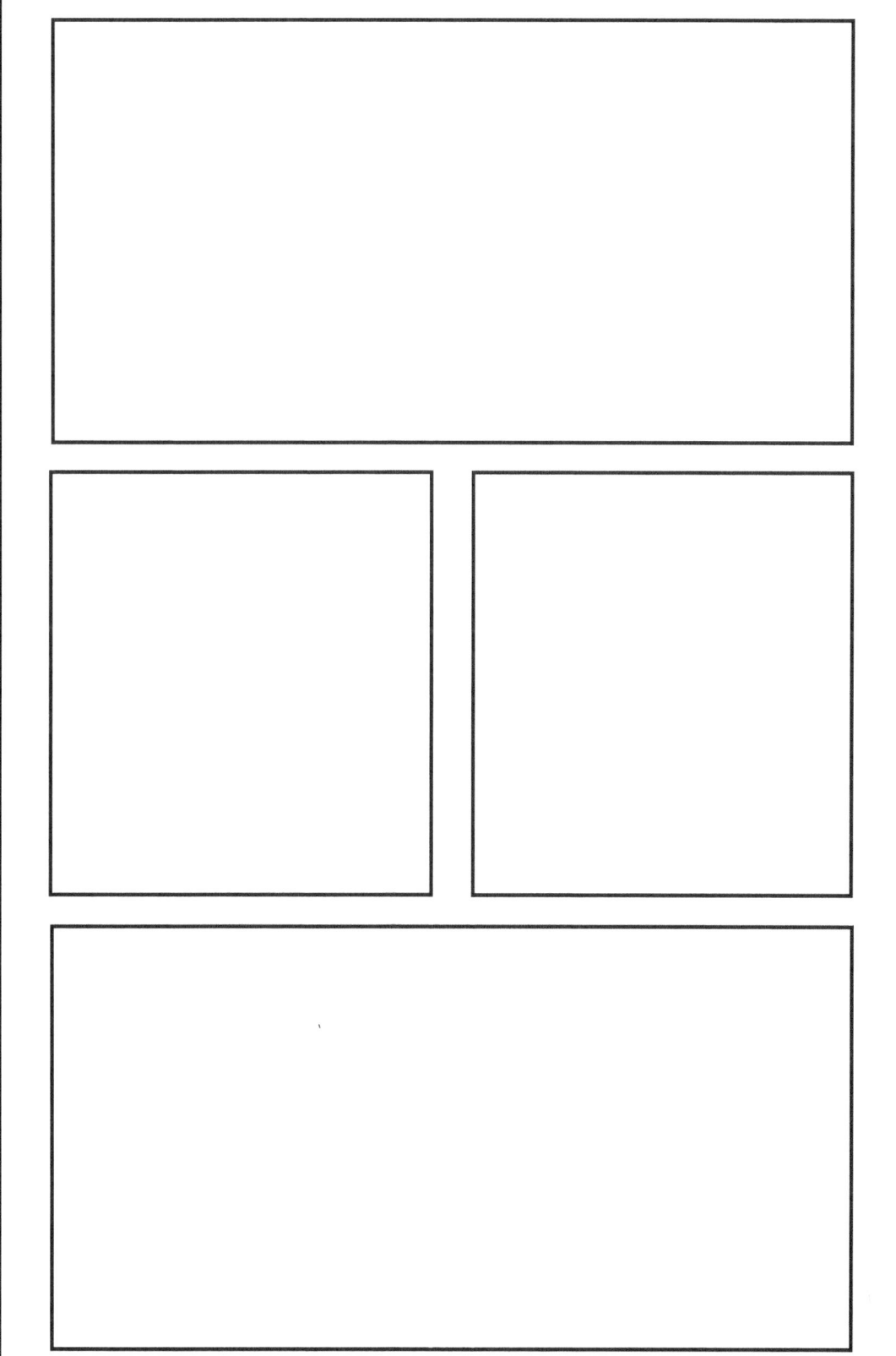

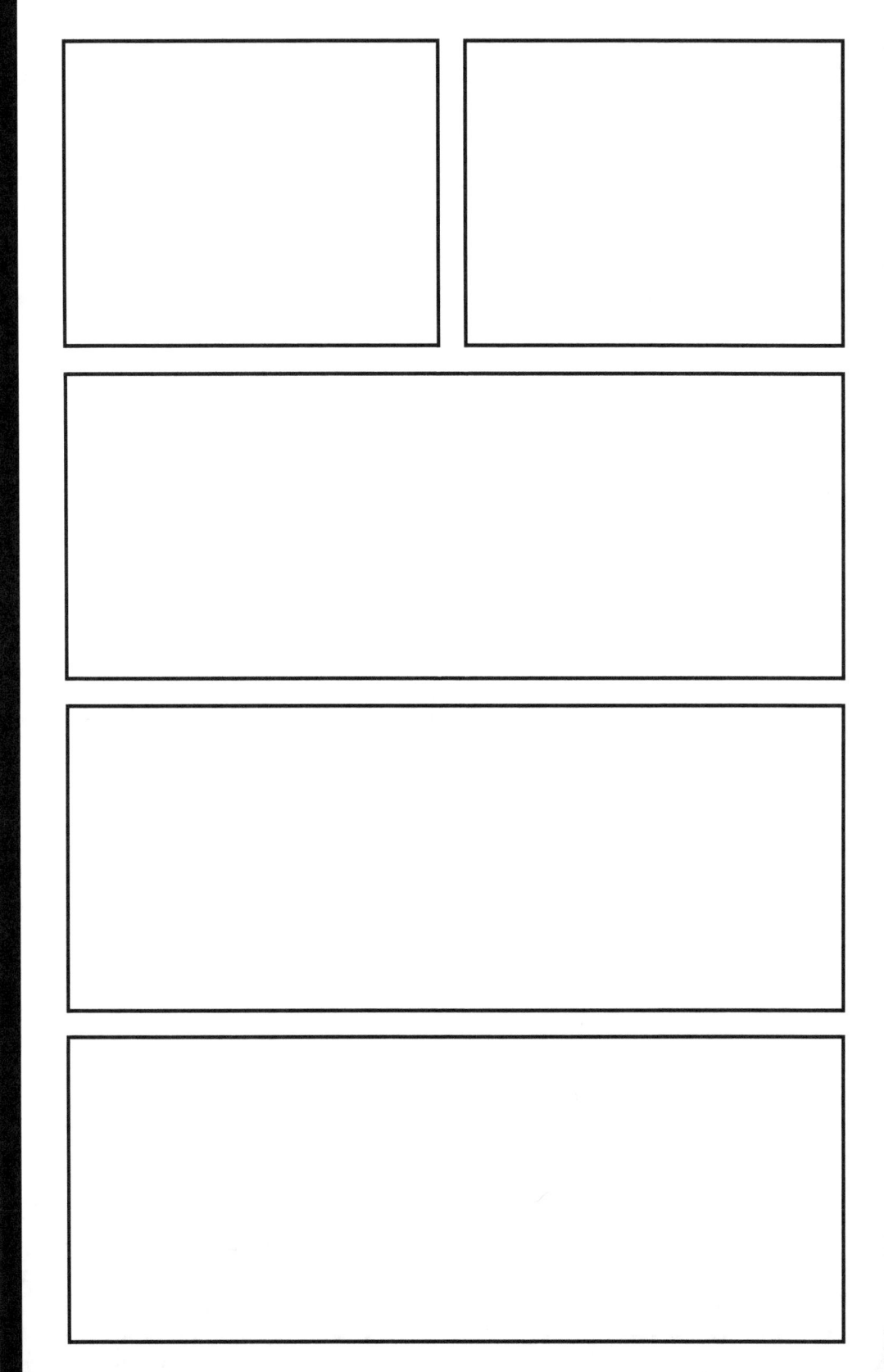

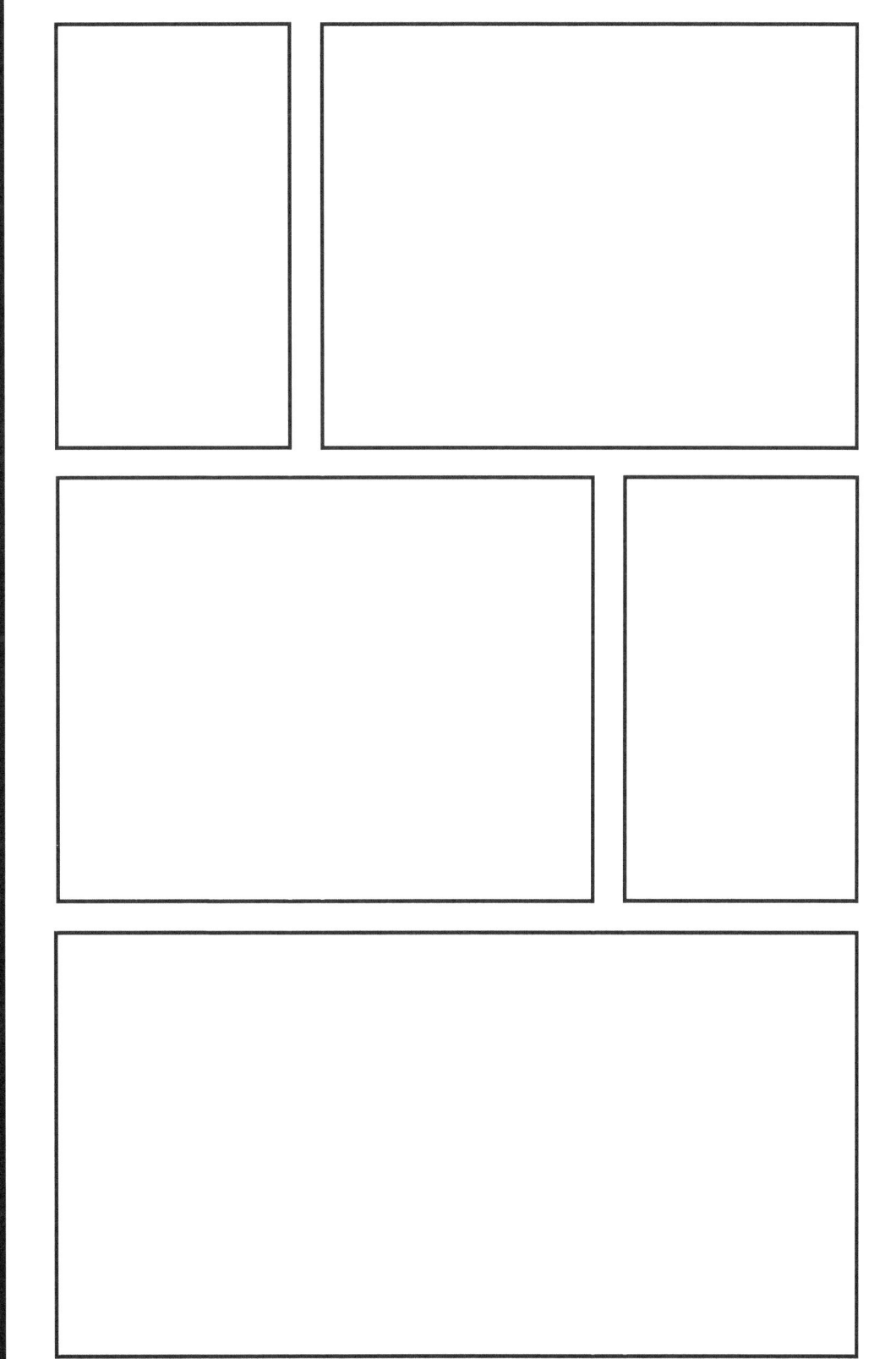

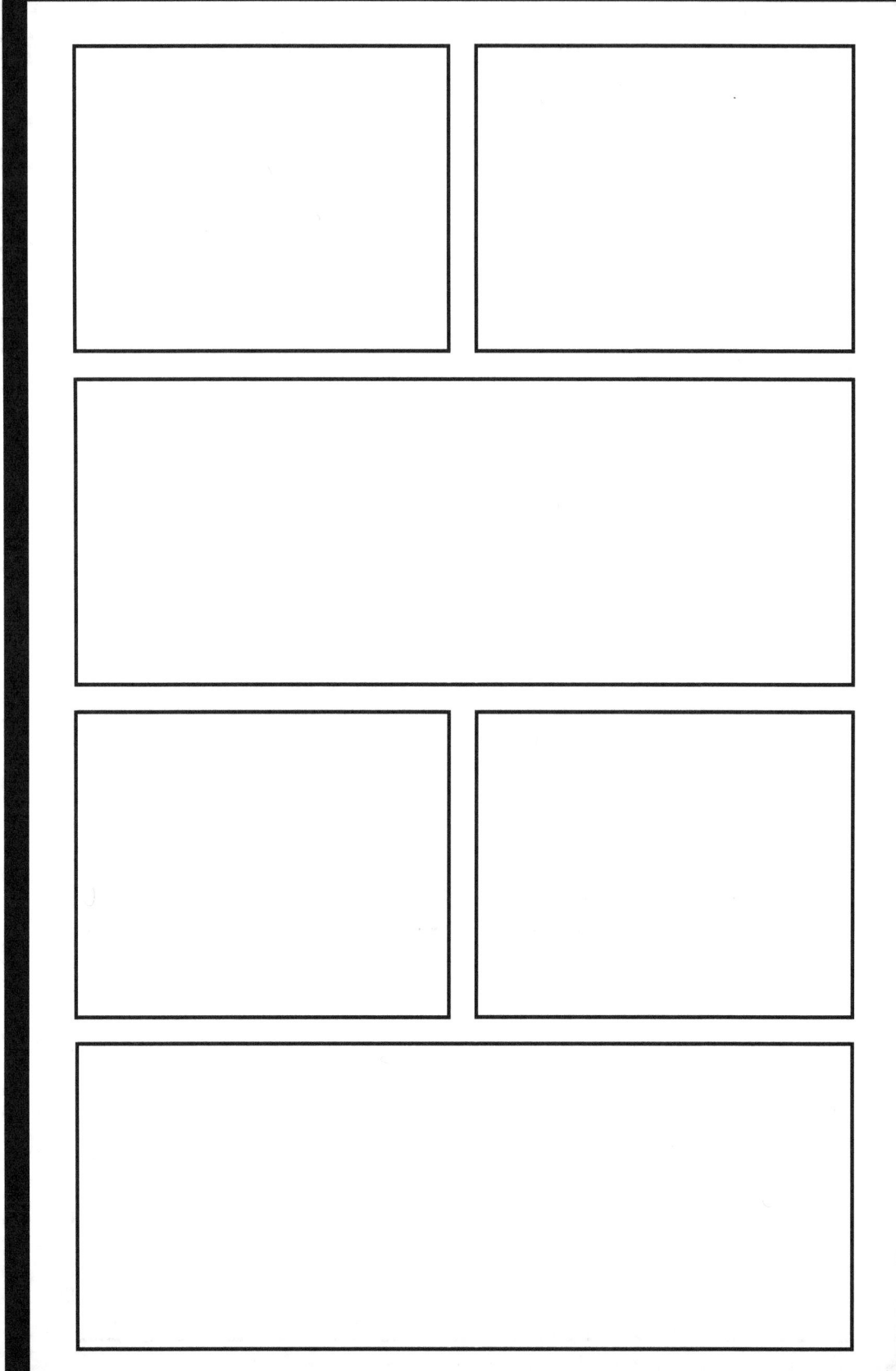

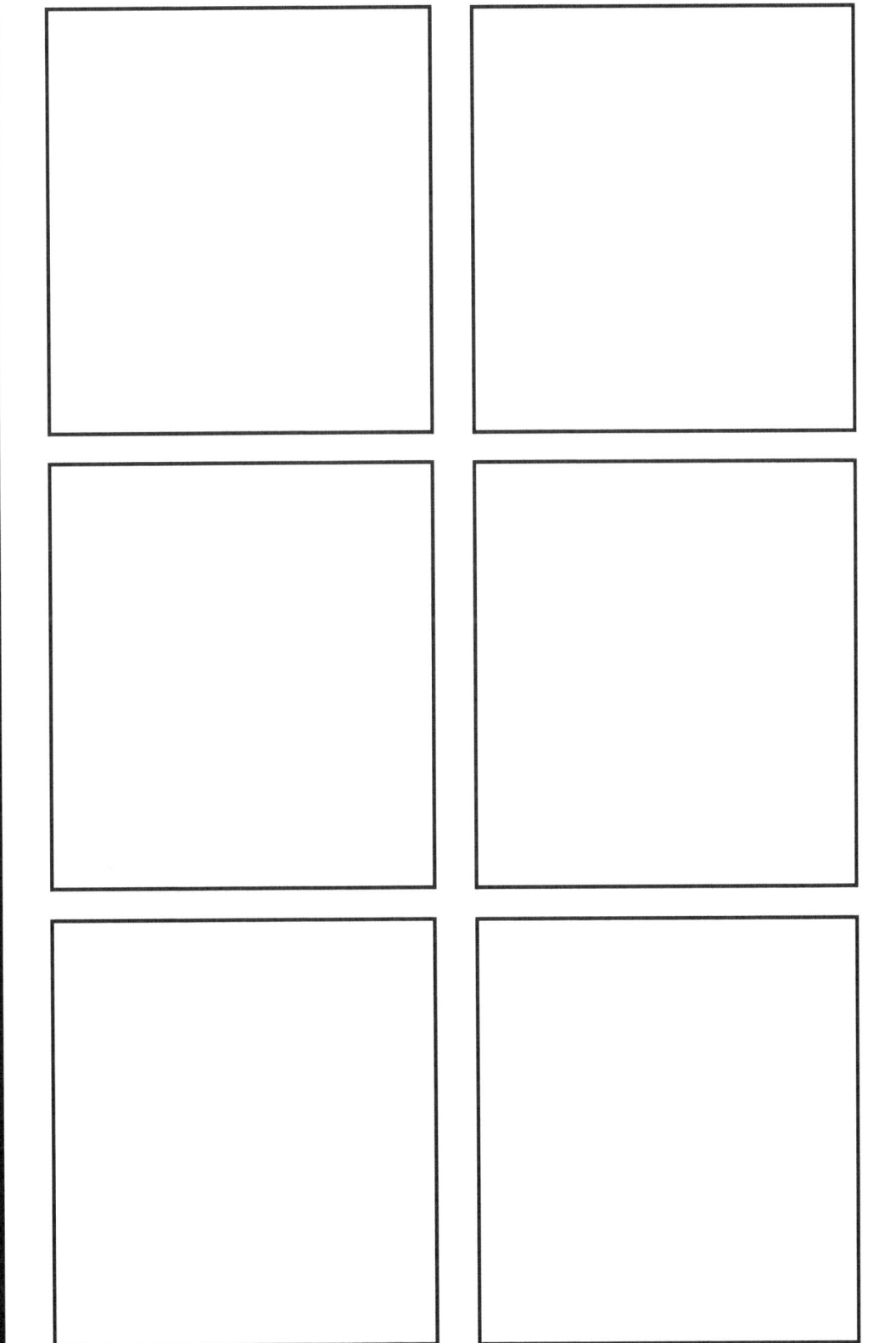

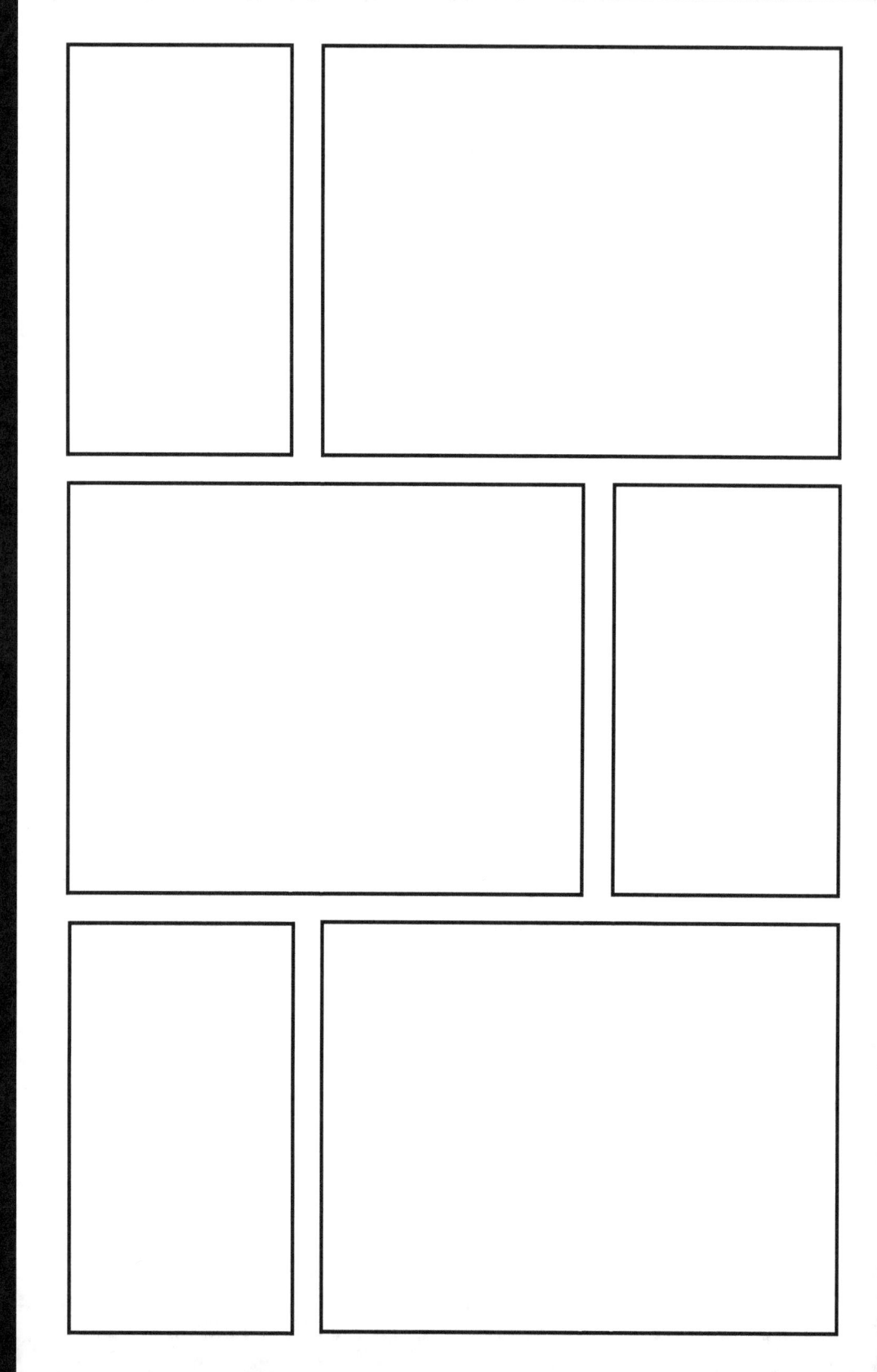

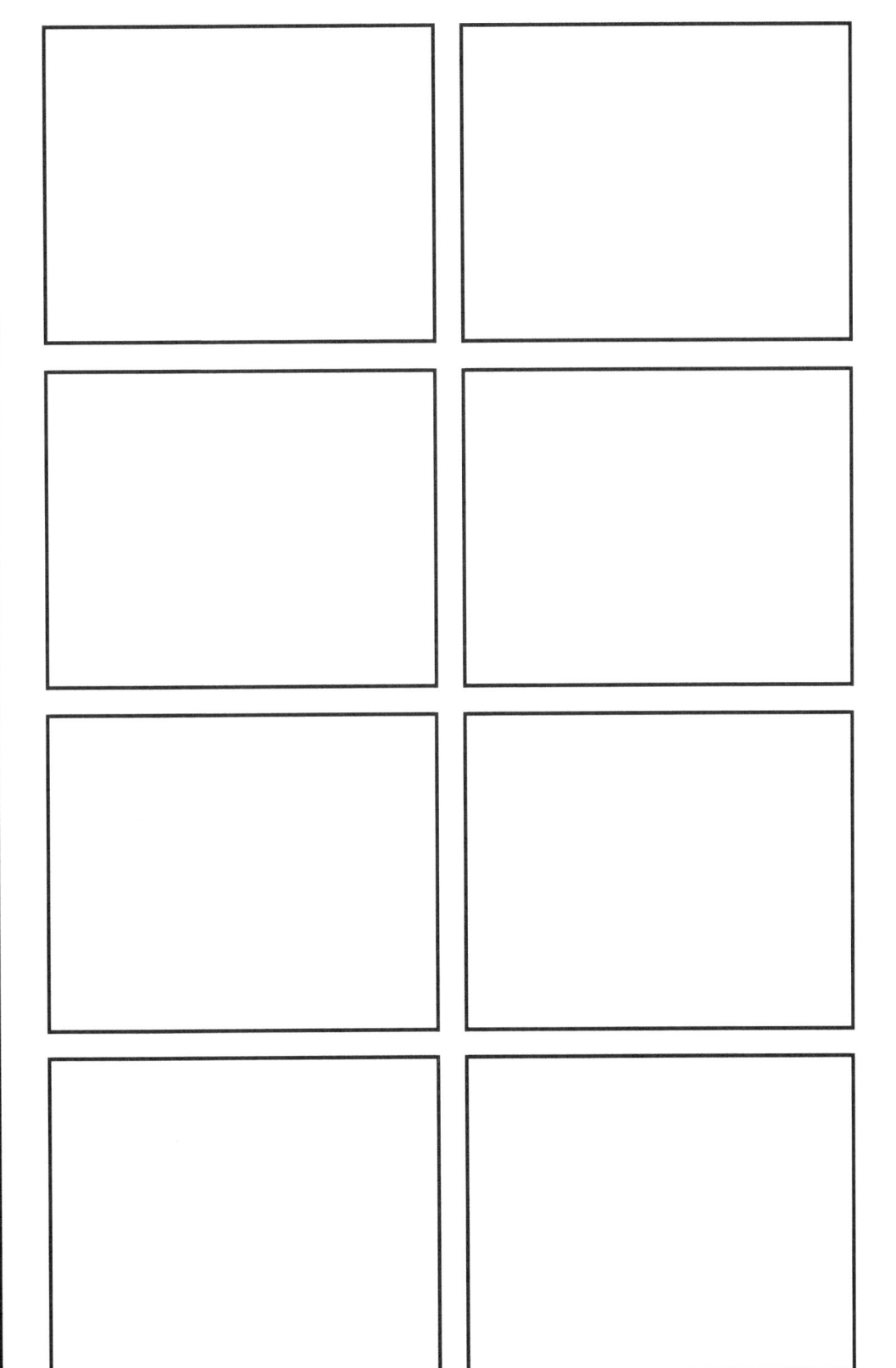

Make your own comic!

Use the following pages to create a special comic and bring it to next year's show. This section has a cover and five interior pages.

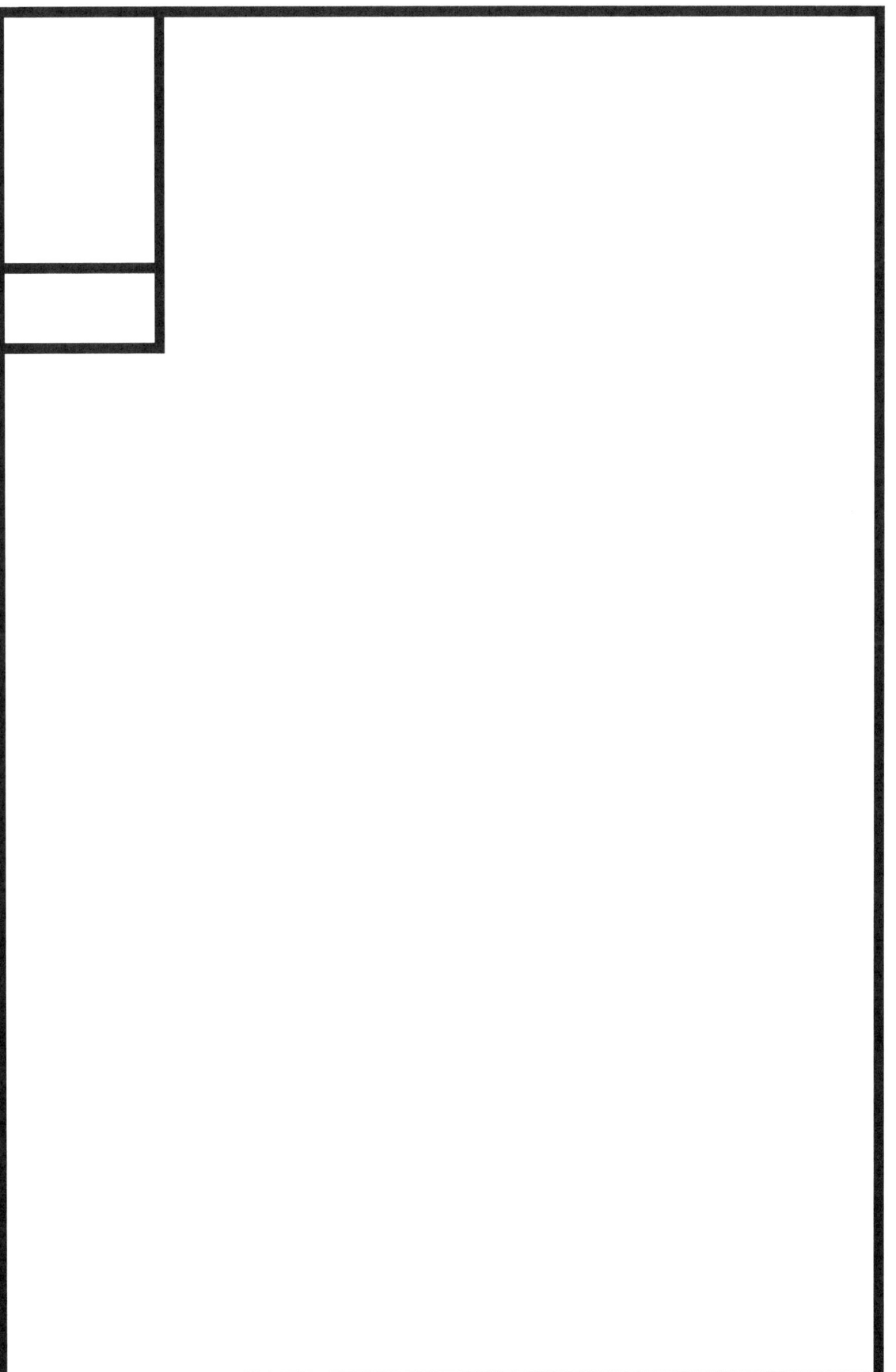

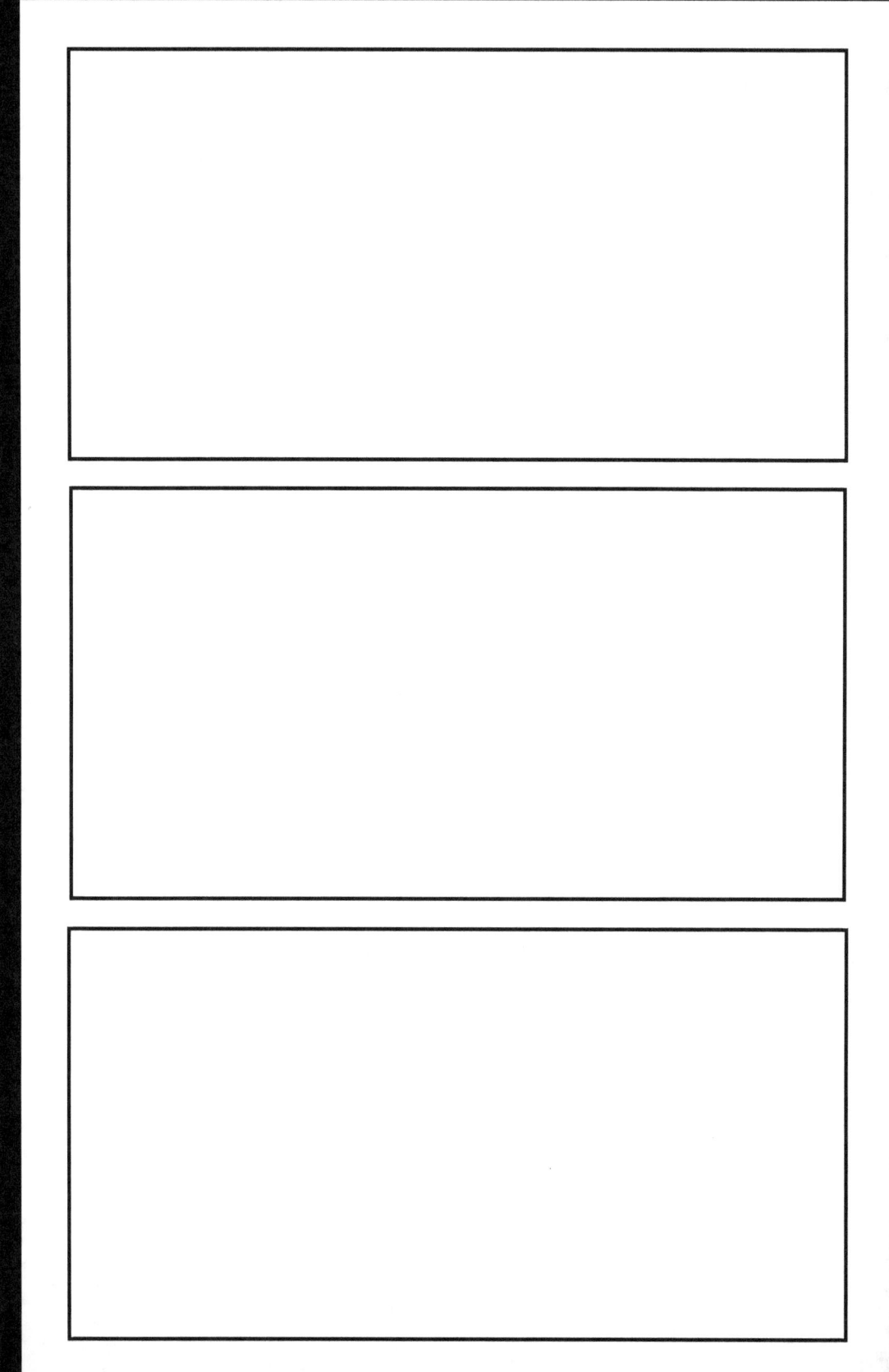

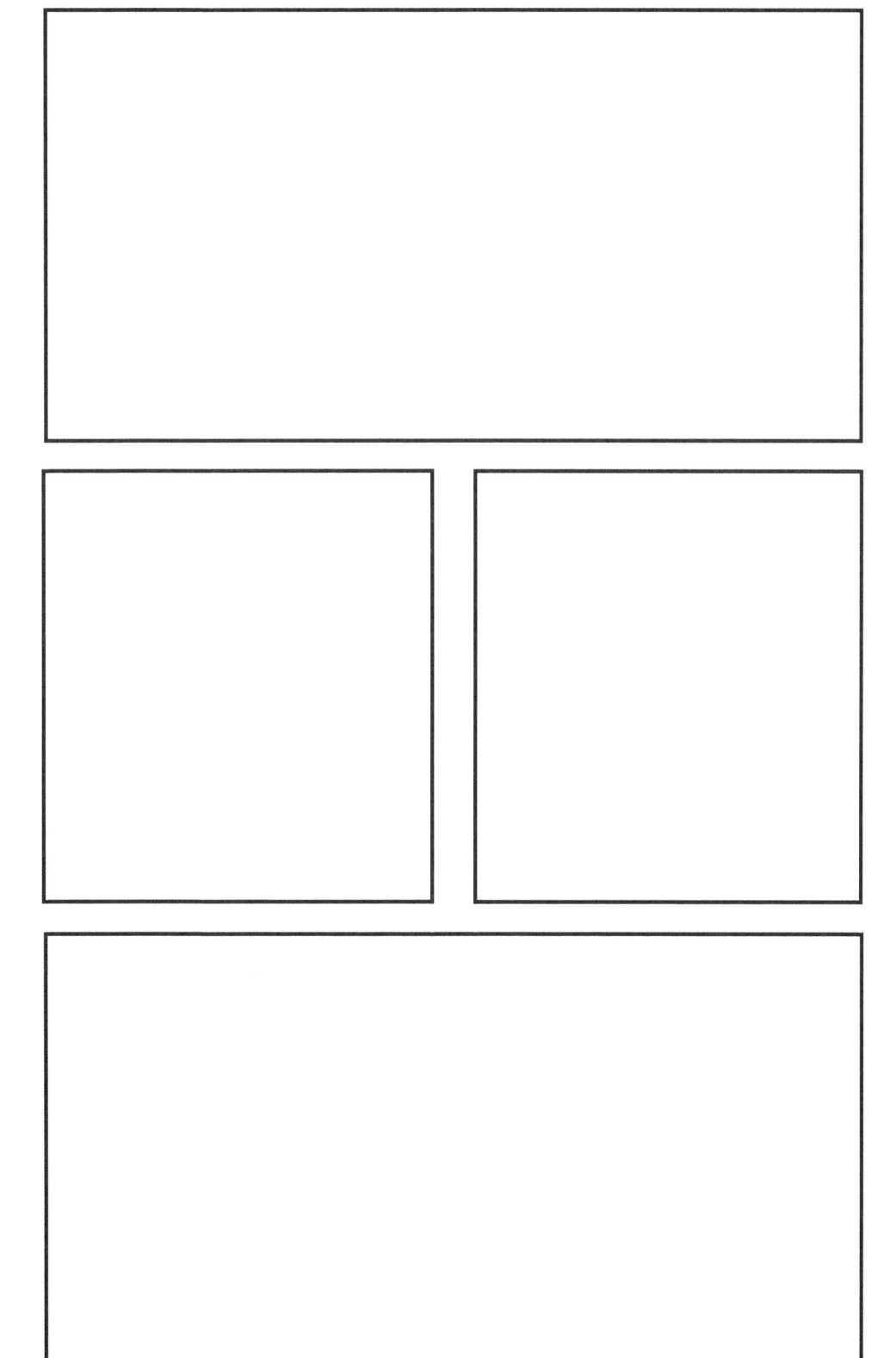

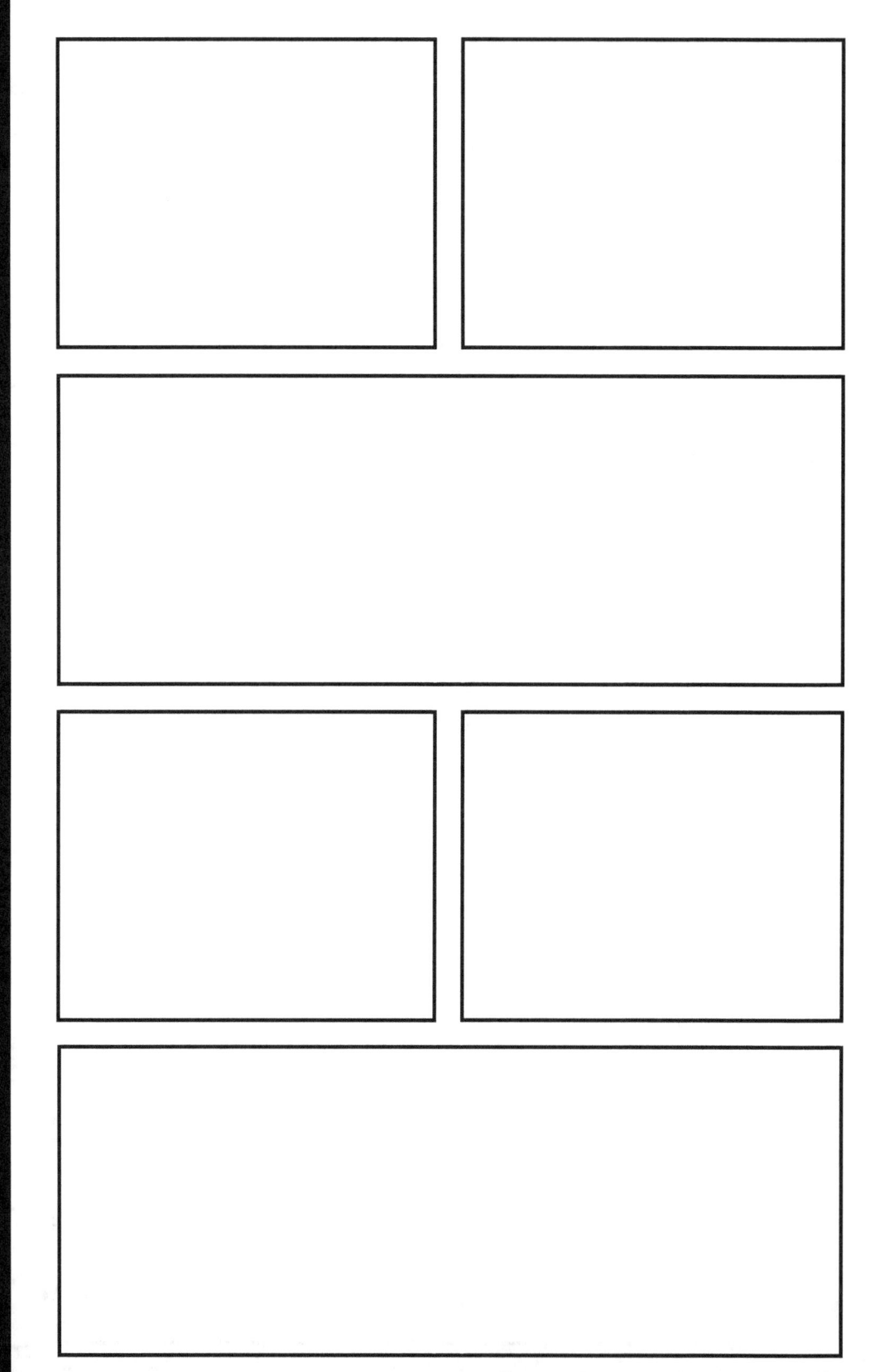

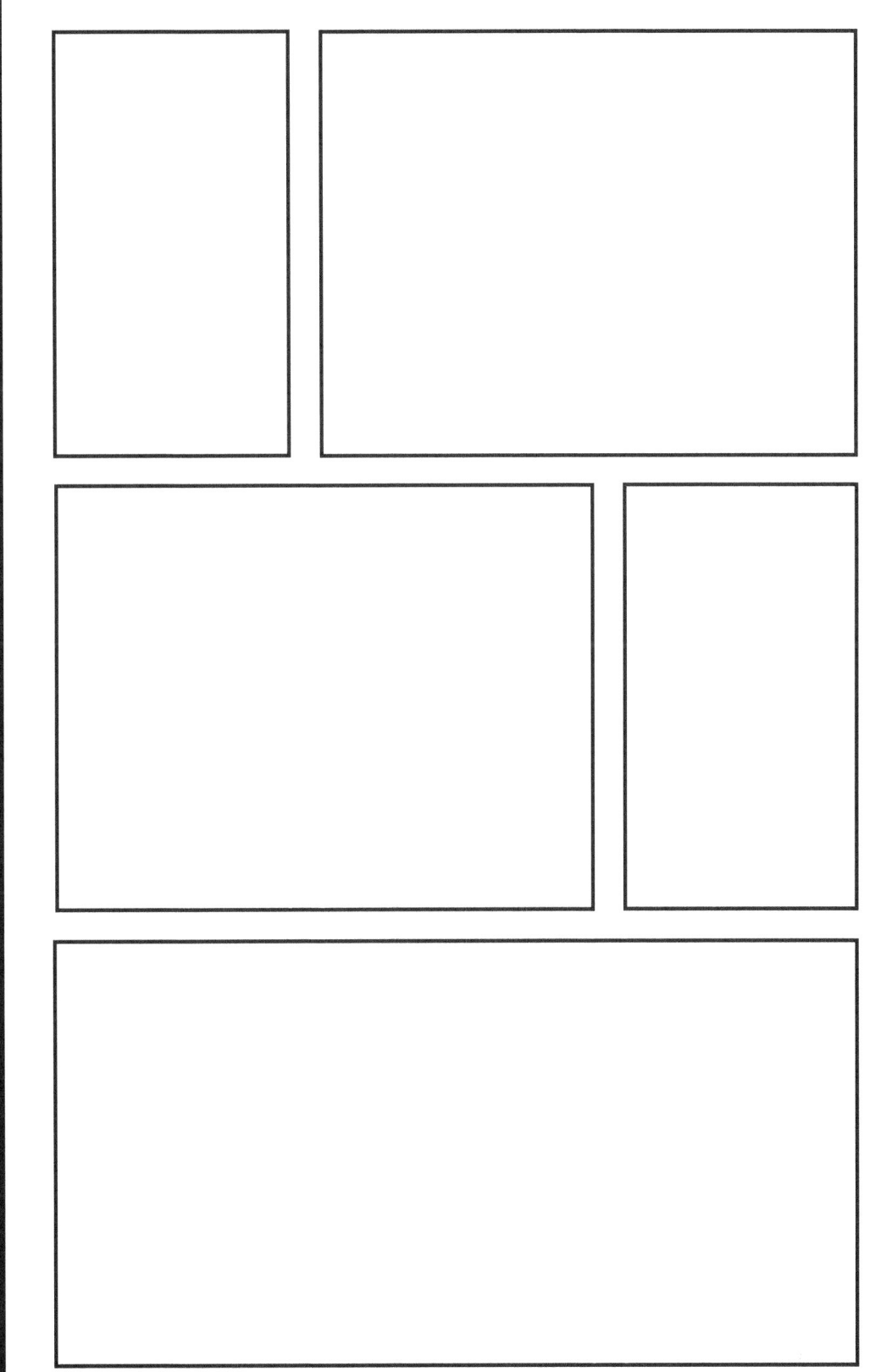

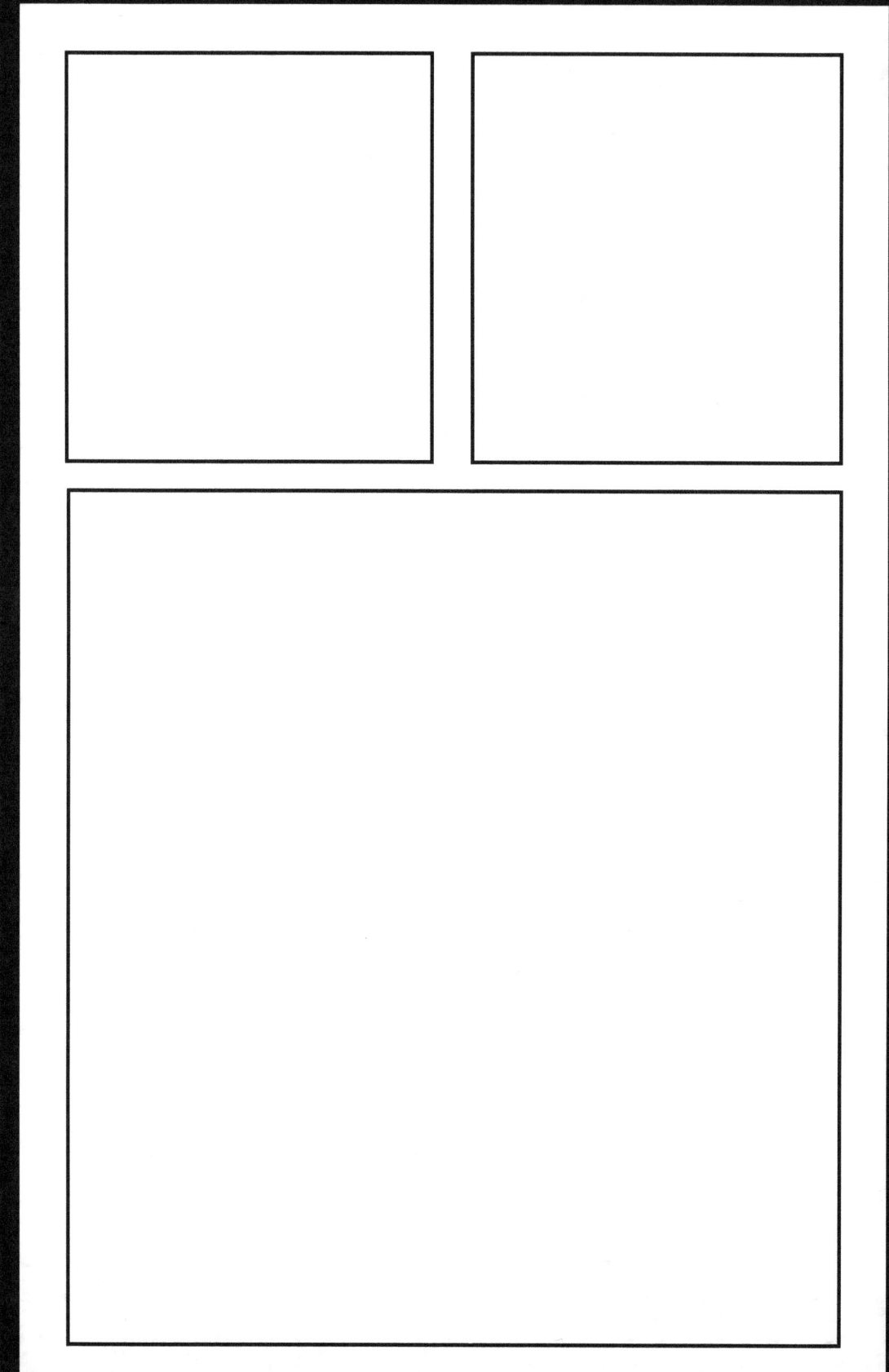

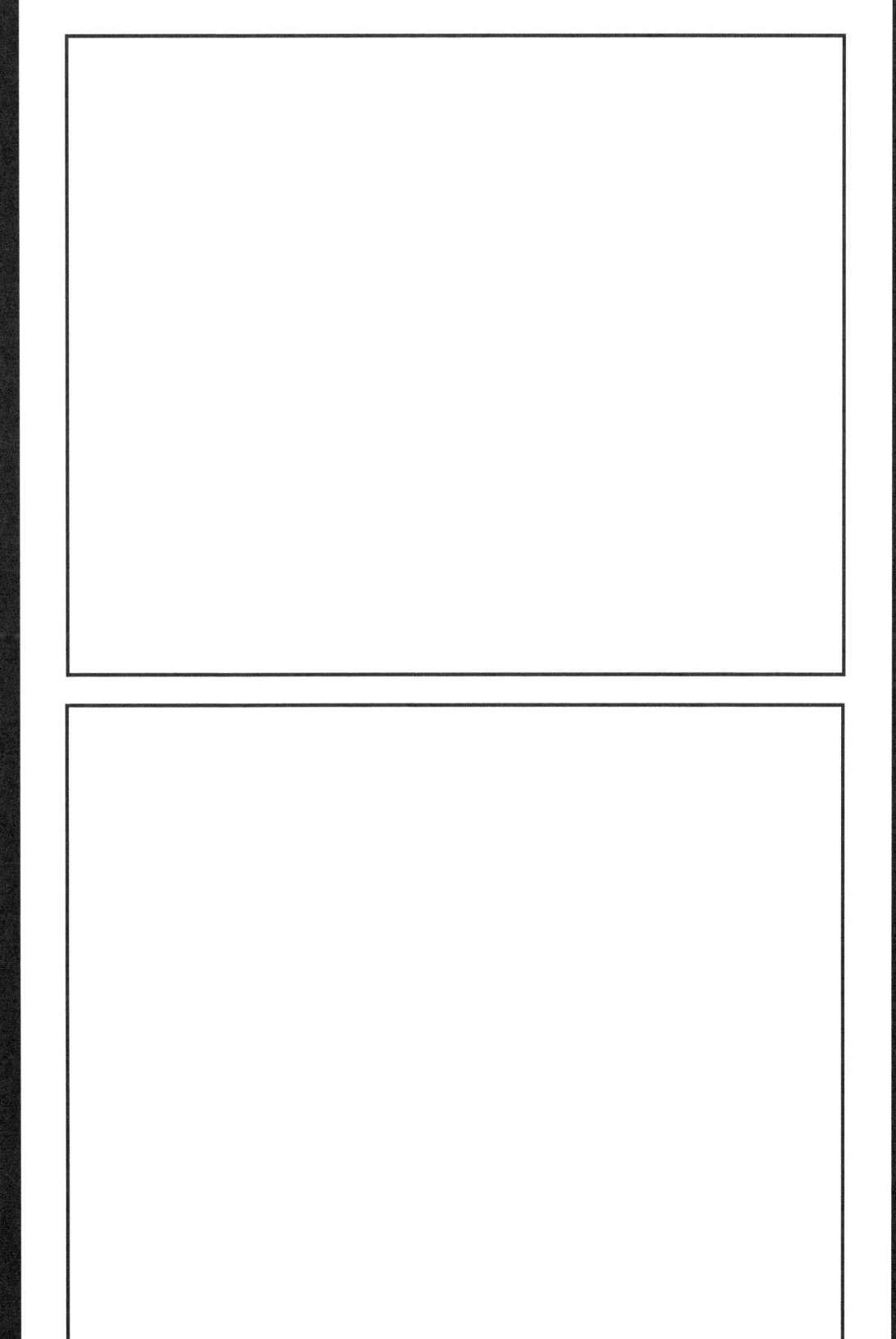

figidpress
Finally I Got it Done!

BOOKS, COMICS, & LEARNING EVENTS

VISIT OUR WEBSITE TO FIND INFORMATION ABOUT UNIQUE BOOKS, COMICS, AND MORE.

WE ARE A PROUD SPONSOR OF

INDYpendent creator show

A LOCAL EVENT IN INDIANAPOLIS THAT PROMOTES CREATIVITY, EDUCATION, NETWORKING, AND GROWTH IN MANY CREATIVE FIELDS.

www.INDYpendentshow.com

www.FIGIDPress.com
FIGIDPress@Gmail.com

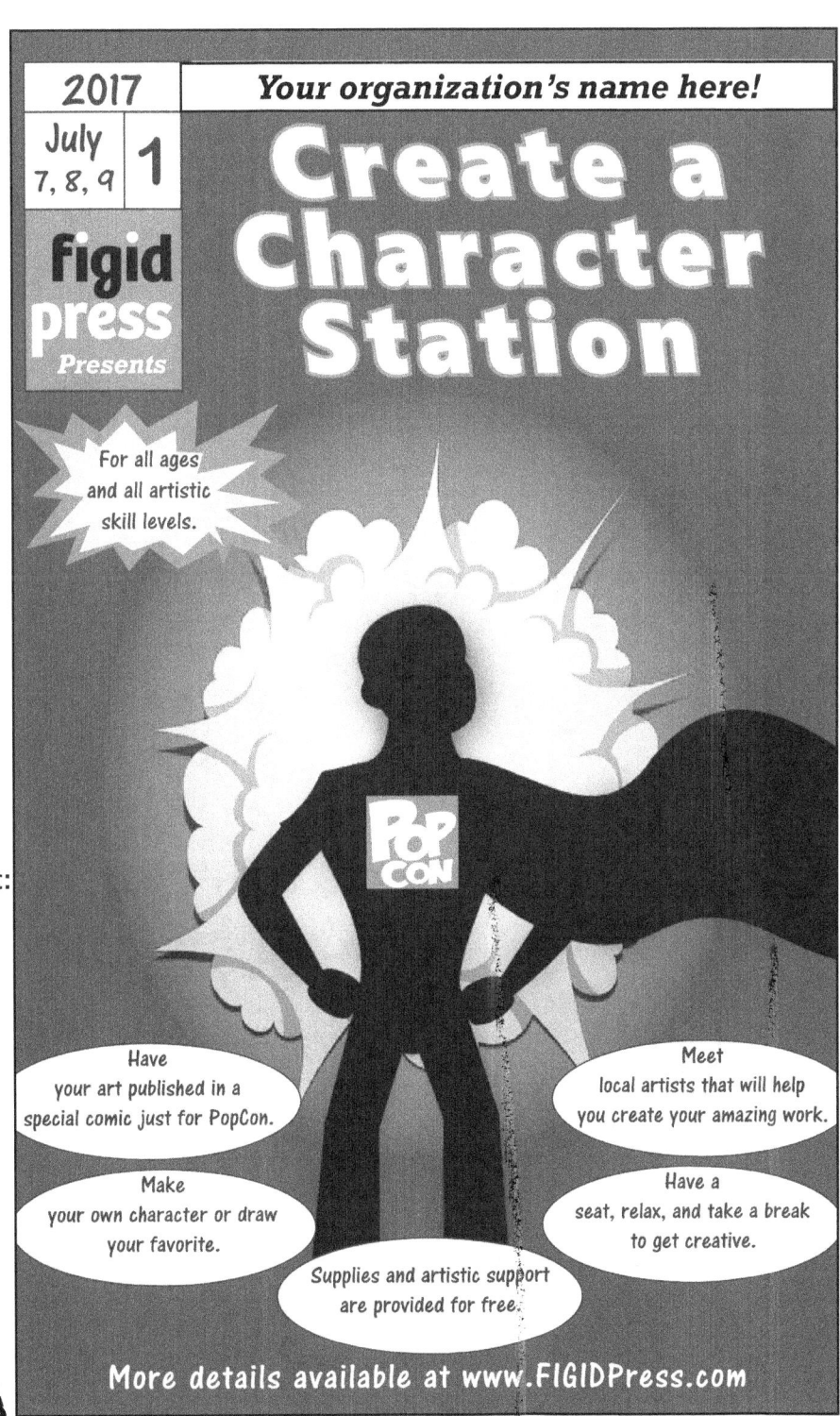

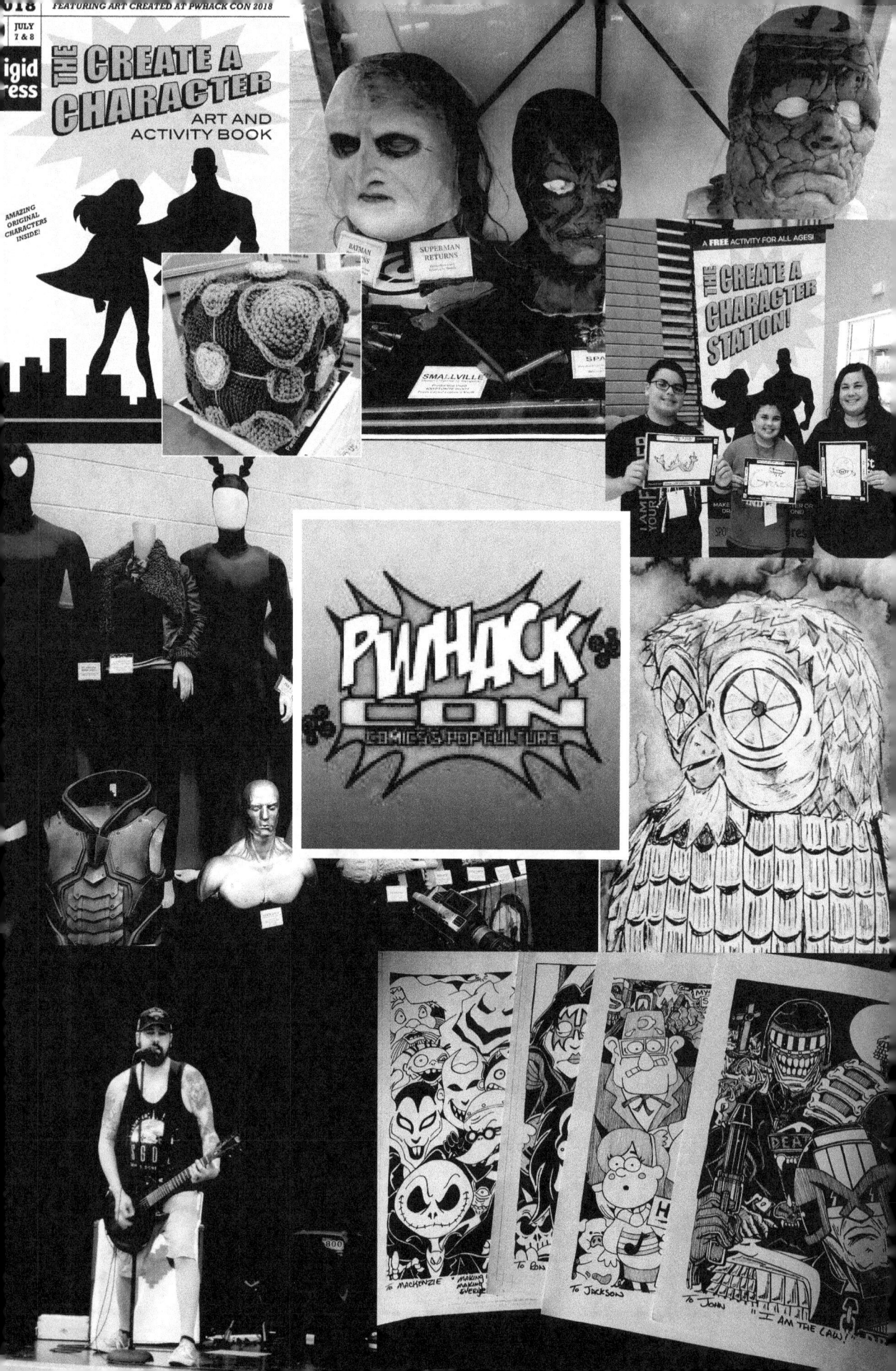

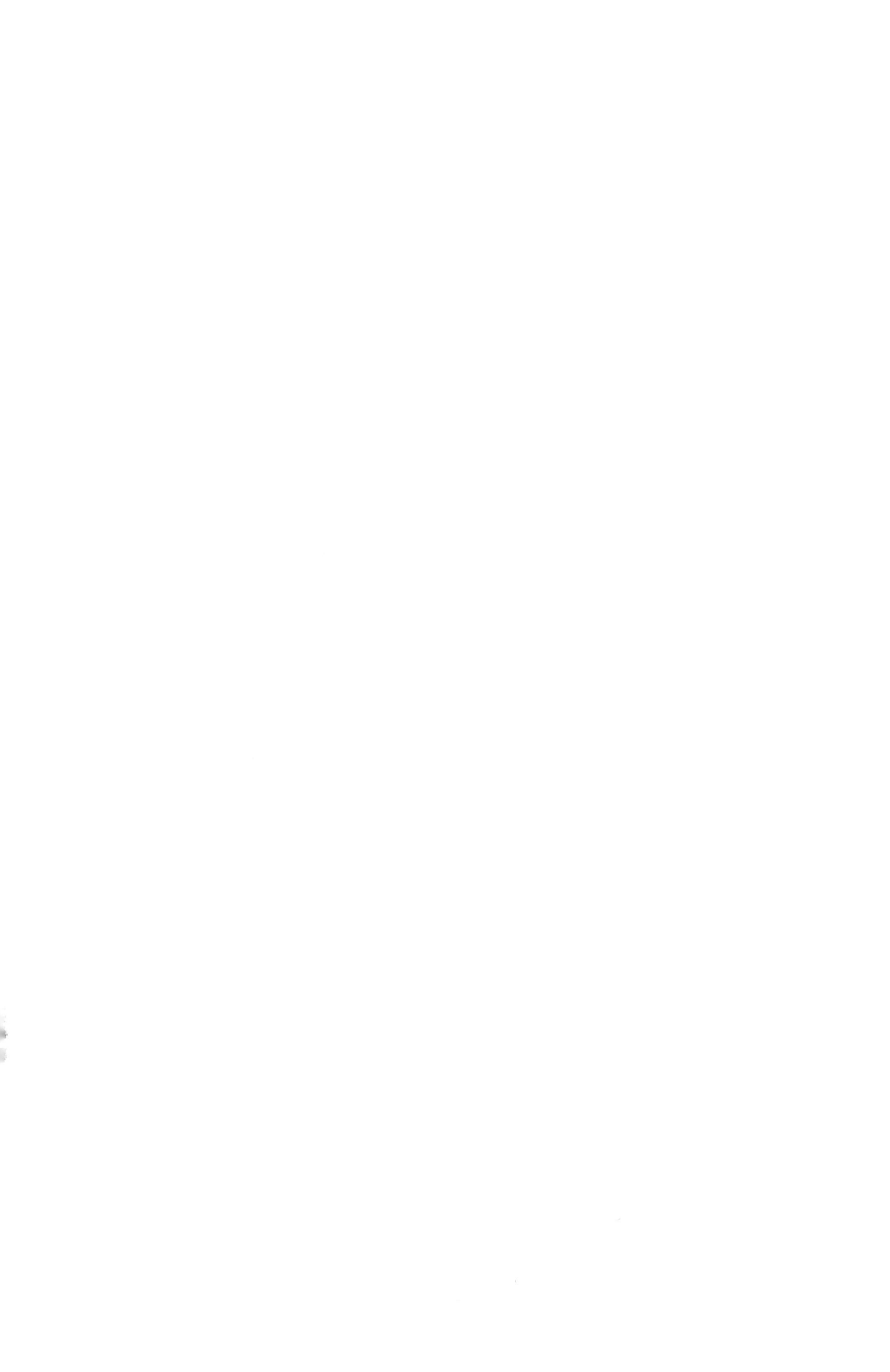

www.ingramcontent.com/pod-product-compliance
Lightning Source LLC
Chambersburg PA
CBHW062334220526
45469CB00008B/2707